W0050231

Siyasi
Muslims

HILAL AHMED

Siyasi Muslims

A Story *of* Political Islams in India

PENGUIN
VIKING
An imprint of Penguin Random House

VIKING

USA | Canada | UK | Ireland | Australia
New Zealand | India | South Africa | China | Singapore

Viking is part of the Penguin Random House group of companies
whose addresses can be found at global.penguinrandomhouse.com

Published by Penguin Random House India Pvt. Ltd
4th Floor, Capital Tower 1, MG Road,
Gurugram 122 002, Haryana, India

Penguin
Random House
India

First published in Viking by Penguin Random House India 2019

Copyright © Hilal Ahmed 2019

ISBN 9780670091409

Typeset in Adobe Caslon Pro by Manipal Digital Systems, Manipal
Printed at Replika Press Pvt. Ltd, India

This book is dedicated to my guru,
Sudipta Kaviraj

Contents

PART III: THE POLITICS OF SIYASI MUSLIMS

List of Abbreviations

- ABMAC: All India Babri Masjid Action Committee
- AIADMK: All India Anna Dravida Munnetra Kazhagam
- AIMIM: All India Majlis-e-Ittehad-ul-Muslimeen
- AIMPLB: All India Muslim Personal Law Board
- AIR: All India Reporter
- AMP: Association of Muslim Professionals
- AMU: Aligarh Muslim University
- BJP: Bharatiya Janata Party
- BJS: Bharatiya Jana Sangh
- BMMA: Bharatiya Muslim Mahila Andolan
- BMMCC: Babri Masjid Movement Coordination Committee
- BSE: Bombay Stock Exchange
- CSDS: Centre for the Study of Developing Societies
- FDI: Foreign Direct Investment
- FPTP: First past the post
- IIM: Indian Institutes of Management
- IMCCI: Indian Muslim Chamber of Commerce and Industry
- JD: Janata Dal
- JD(U): Janata Dal (United)
- JIH: Jamaat-e-Islami Hind
- JP: Janata Party
- MCQ: Multiple choice question

- MOTN: Mood of the Nation
- NCM: National Commission for Minorities
- NCMEI: National Commission for Minority Educational Institutions
- NDA: National Democratic Alliance
- NES: National Election Studies
- NIC: National Integration Council
- NSS: National Sample Survey
- NSSO: National Sample Survey Office
- OBC: Other Backward Classes
- PBUH: Peace be upon him
- PR: Proportional representation (system)
- RJD: Rashtriya Janata Dal
- RSS: Rashtriya Swayamsevak Sangh
- SC: Scheduled Caste
- SCR: Supreme Court Reports
- ST: Scheduled Tribe
- UCC: Uniform Civil Code
- UPA: United Progressive Alliance
- VHP: Vishwa Hindu Parishad

Acknowledgements

This book would not have been possible without the institutional and intellectual support provided by the Centre for the Study of Developing Societies (CSDS)—popularly known as the 'Centre' in the world of Indian social sciences.

The work benefited immensely from conversations with my colleagues at CSDS. I am grateful to Ashis Nandy, V.B. Singh, D.L. Sheth, Shail Mayaram, Rajeev Bhargava, Peter Ronald deSouza, Sanjeer Alam, Sanjay Kumar, Aditya Nigam, Abhay Kumar Dubey, Awadhendra Sharan, Prathama Banerjee, Priyadarshini Vijaisri, Rakesh Pandey, Ravi Sundaram, Ravi Vasudevan, Ravi Kant, Praveen Rai, Ananya Vajpeyi, Prabhat Kumar, Nishikant Kolge and Baidik Bhattacharya for their comments, criticisms and encouragement.

I am also grateful to our Lokniti team: Dhananjay Kumar Singh, Vibha Atri, Jyoti Mishra, Shreyas Sardesai, Rishikesh Yadav, Babita, Gayatri, Amrit Negi, Amrit Pandey and Anurag Jain, and the CSDS library and staff: Avinash Jha, Jaysree Jayanathan, K.A.Q.A. Hilal, Himanshu, Ghanshyam, Harsh, R. Natrajan, Jagdish, Ranjeet Negi, Manoj, Ayodhya Verma and others for their support.

Intellectual discussions with Rama Lakshmi, Madhulika Banerjee, Suhas Palshikar, Sandeep Shastri, Maulana Syed Athar Hussain Delhvai, S. Irfan Habib, Sanjay Pugalia, Arfa

Khanam Shervani, Urmilesh, Rakhshanda Jalil, Syeda Hameed, Badri Narayan, Faizan Mustafa, Apoorvanand, Rahul Verma, Ravish Kumar, Manoj Jha, Nilanjana Kaviraj, Shahid Siddiqui, Nivedita Menon, Jamal Malik, Vivek Shukla, Rana Safvi, Kumar Prashant, Iqbal Ahmad, Irfan Ahmed, Nilanjan Mukhopadhyay, Ira Bhaskar, Vinod Sharma, Satish Deshpande, Mary John, Tani Bhargava, Pratap Bhanu Mehta, Mahesh Rangrajan, Rahul Dev, Farah Naqvi, Purushottam Agarwal, Shamsul Islam, Manorajan Mohanty, Gilles Verniers, M.A.A. Khan, Yashaswini Chandra, Shailja Sharma, M. Ghazali Khan, Manish Jain, Kavita Singh, Riaz Ahmad, Afroz Alam, Khalid Anis Ansari, Tamanna, Inamdar and, above all, my ustad, M.N. Thakur, have always been very helpful in shaping my arguments. I am thankful to them.

I always admire the courage, political honesty and intellectual sharpness of Yogendra Yadav. His creative ideas have contributed a lot to my intellectual life. I do not have adequate words to express my gratitude for him.

I thank Vikram Nayak for his friendship, dedication and faith in me. His creative engagements always encourage me to work hard. I am also grateful for all the illustrations and cartoons he made especially for this book.

I also give thanks to all my students, especially those who attended the CSDS teaching programmes—*Researching the Contemporary* and *Mainstream and the Margins*—for their intellectual contribution.

I am glad to acknowledge the support I received from my family. I would like to thank my wife, Nazima Parveen, for her unconditional love, support and, above all, intellectual comradeship as a friend and partner. She has always been a source of inspiration for me. I have learnt a lot from her. She is my conscience keeper.

My children—Sarmad, Maaz and Raheel—contribute to my personal and intellectual life in their own ways. I am thankful to their comments and criticisms and the adjustments they make to accommodate my unusual working schedule. My sincere thanks to Penguin Random House India for recognizing the significance of this subject. I am particularly grateful to Premanka Goswami and Rachita Raj for their support and encouragement.

This book is dedicated to my guru, Sudipta Kaviraj, one of the best minds India has ever produced. He taught me the political significance of honest intellectual labour.

Hilal Ahmed
March 2019
New Delhi

FAQs: Muslims and Politics

1. How do we make sense of the Muslims of India? We are often told that they are highly diversified and plural, while at the same time they are treated as a homogeneous community, especially in political terms. Is this not self-contradictory?

This is a legitimate question. And this book tries to offer a way out. It addresses Muslims not as numbers but as a constitutional category, a religious minority and as a collectivity in two different senses.

I see Muslims as a collectivity in a *positive* sense, when individuals with Muslim names and/or groups, who prefer to call themselves Islamic, are recognized as the beneficiary of constitutionally granted rights, such as the right to profess religion and the right to protect culture and heritage.

However, I see Muslims as a collectivity in a *negative* sense, particularly when individuals with Muslim names and legally recognized minority institutions with Islamic contents are threatened and attacked, especially by Hindutva essentialists. In both cases, Muslimness is produced as an undifferentiated entity. We are forced to imagine Muslims as one homogeneous community. This book is an attempt to demonstrate that Muslims are divided on caste, class and regional lines, which actually determine their politics.

2. Is Muslim politics all about Muslim voting behaviour in elections?

No. Electoral politics is just one form of Muslim politics. This book tries to capture other types of Muslim political engagement as well.

3. Do Muslims always vote strategically?

Yes and no. Muslims, like other communities, vote as a group at the constituency level. But there is no evidence which suggests that there is a national Muslim vote bank. In this book, we actually explore the idea of the vote bank as a metaphor of Muslim politics. (See Chapter 9.)

4. Are Muslim religious institutions—mosques and madrasas— directly involved in politics? Do they instruct Muslims to vote strategically in all elections?

It would be wrong to make a sweeping generalization in this regard. In some cases, Muslim religious organizations directly advise Muslims to vote for a particular candidate or party at the local level. Certain organizations, such as the All India Muslim Majlis-e-Mushwarat, and certain individuals, such as the imam of Jama Masjid of Delhi, also issue election appeals. Interestingly, these organizations and individuals are approached by political parties, including the BJP, for favourable statements. In fact, the imam of Jama Masjid issued an election fatwa in favour of the BJP in 2004 (see image on p. xxii).

5. Why do Muslims not participate in secular political activities?

This is not correct. Actually, Muslims are always recognized only as Muslims. Their active participation in secular politics is ignored. It is very important to realize the fact that Muslims, like any other community in India, participate in all forms of politics without giving up their identities.

6. Are there any unwritten norms of Muslim politics in India?

Yes, there are three such norms of Muslim politics in India, which are followed by all Muslim political groups. First, there is a strong adherence to legal–constitutional discourse. Muslims' demands are always articulated in a language of rights and laws. Second, there is an emphasis on 'Muslim contribution' in the process of nation-building. Third, there is an idea of 'Muslim unity', which is always highlighted to assert constitutionally recognized minority rights.

7. What are 'Muslim issues'?

There is this media-driven imagination of a package called Muslim issues. Debatable issues of Islamic identity are called Muslim issues. Hence, the Babri Masjid in Ayodhya, the protection of Muslim personal law, the protection of the minority status of Jamia Millia Islamia and Aligarh Muslim University, the protection of Urdu and, lately, the inclusion of Muslim Dalits in the Scheduled Caste (SC) list are treated as Muslim issues.

8. Why are Muslims only concerned with their own interests?

This is not true. The Centre for the Study of Developing Societies (CSDS)-Lokniti surveys show that Muslim communities recognize unemployment, poverty and the lack of educational facilities as serious concerns of everyday life. Muslim assertions of this kind are never recorded and discussed in public discourse.

9. Are they really nationalists?

This is an important question. But can we think of a yardstick to measure one's nationalism? I have tried to engage with this question in the chapter on Hindutva and Muslims in the book.

10. What is 'political Islam(s)'? Is it about violence and jihad?

I use the term 'political Islam' to underline the ways in which Islamic principles are reshaped by postcolonial, secular Indian political processes, such as elections. Since there is no one single form of Islam that prevails in India, the term 'political Islam' is used in a plural sense. The chapter on Islamization in postcolonial India deals with this issue in detail.

Violent, jihadi Islam, in my view, is just one form of political Islam. I do not find it relevant with regard to Muslim politics in India.

11. Do Indian Muslims admire ISIS or Al-Qaida–type political movements?

Indian Muslims comprise 18 crore people in this country. How could one make a claim on behalf of this huge and highly diversified population? That said, there is no evidence which suggests that the Muslims of India *admire* ISIS-type organizations. However, the symbolic presence of these global jihadi entities is always used to nurture anti-Muslim discourse in India.

12. Why have they formed the Indian Mujahideen?

Like I mentioned previously, we do not have the adequate resources to really know more about organizations such as the Indian

Mujahideen. In my view, media reports and official statements cannot be used as the ultimate source for any systematic study of Islamic radicalism in India. I have tried to discuss the symbolism of radical Islam in relation to other forms of Muslim politics in this book.

13. Why don't they accept that Kashmir is an integral part of India?

The Kashmir dispute began as a regional movement in the 1980s. Gradually, it transformed into an Islamic issue. Direct support from Pakistan to militant organizations in the 1990s is responsible for this. Interestingly, however, postcolonial Muslim leadership did not recognize the Kashmir dispute as a Muslim issue. Actually, the Kashmir dispute goes against the norms of Muslim politics!

14. Why do they want to follow sharia laws?

This is a media-driven question! CSDS-Lokniti surveys show that Muslims are not even aware of the idea of sharia itself. Muslim communities follow a highly localized set of norms and rules to manage their everyday lives, which are often described as 'gair sharia', or anti-sharia, by the ulema. The chapter on triple talaq goes into this issue in detail.

15. What is the role of the All India Muslim Personal Law Board (AIMPLB)? Is it not a separatist body?

The AIMPLB is not a Muslim representative organization. Muslims do not elect the office bearers of the AIMPLB. It is a registered NGO established by the Muslim religious elite in 1972.

No, it cannot be called a separatist body as it follows the legal principles set out by the Constitution itself. In fact, the Supreme

Court also recognizes the legitimate existence of the AIMPLB as an NGO and/or as a Muslim advisory body in one of its judgements.

16. What is the problem with singing 'Vande Mataram' and/or chanting the slogan 'Bharat Mata ki Jai'?

These questions come from the Hindutva imagination of Muslimness. I have discussed these aspects in Chapter 4.

17. What is the problem with the Ram temple in Ayodhya? Why don't the Muslims give it to the Hindus?

The Ram Temple–Babri Masjid dispute is not a Hindu–Muslim issue. It is a dispute between three parties over a 2.77-acre land, which was acquired by the government in 1993. Since common Muslims and Hindus are not the stakeholders in this case, there is no point in debating this question.

18. What is the role of Muslim organizations, such as the All India Majlis-e-Ittehad-ul-Muslimeen (AIMIM) of Asaduddin Owaisi, the Jamaat-e-Islami and the Jamiat Ulama-e-Hind, in contemporary Indian politics?

The AIMIM is a political party, while the Jamaat-e-Islami and the Jamiat Ulama-e-Hind are the Muslim pressure groups. Hence, they are bound to perform very different functions. As a political party, the AIMIM contests elections and makes coalitions in legislative bodies, while Muslim pressure groups create channels to engage with the government on issues that they call 'Muslim issues'. The book discusses these forms of engagements in various chapters.

I recognize the fact that Asaduddin Owaisi has nurtured his image as a religiously committed, modern, secular Muslim leader of the country. However, I strongly feel that his politics does not deviate from the three unwritten norms of Muslim politics, which I have discussed in this book.

19. Why do Muslims oppose the BJP? What is their problem with Narendra Modi?

This is not true. On an average, 6–7 per cent of Muslims vote for the BJP at the national level. This went up to 9 per cent in 2014. This reflects the diversity of Muslim politics.

In 2014, there was a tacit acceptance of Narendra Modi among Muslims. But he himself tried to cultivate the perception that Muslims hate him and do not vote in his name! It has helped him in consolidating the BJP's pro-Hindutva constituency in the post-2014 scenario.

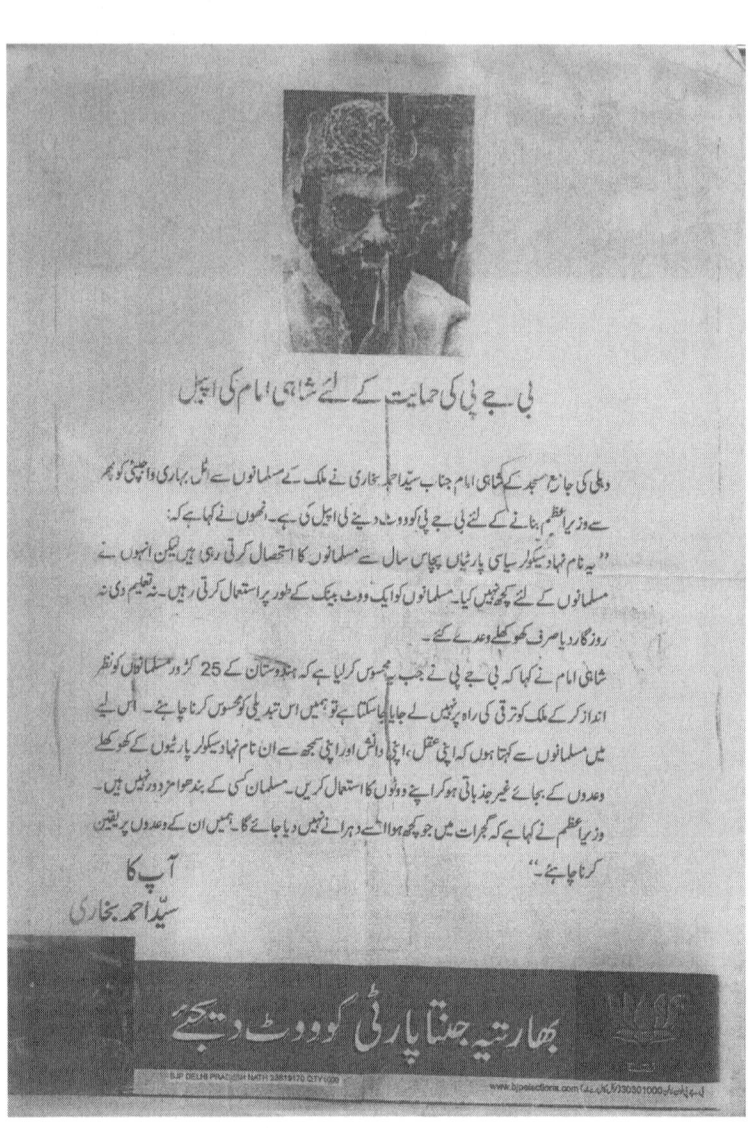

Source: Hilal Ahmed.

बी जे पी की हिमायत के लिए शाही इमाम की अपील

दिल्ली की जामा मस्जिद के शाही इमाम सय्यद अहमद बुखारी ने मुल्क के मुसलमानों से अटल बिहारी वाजपेयी को फिर से वजीर ए आजम बनाने के लिए बी जे पी को वोट देने की अपील की है। उन्होने कहा है कि ये नामनिहाद सेकुलर सियासी पार्टियां 50 साल से मुसलमानों का इस्तहसाल करती रहीं हैं। लेकिन उन्होने मुसलमानों के लिए कुछ नहीं किया। मुसलमानो को एक वोट बैंक के तौर पर इस्तेमाल करते रहे। न तालीम दी न रोजगार दिया, सिर्फ खोखले वादे किए। शाही इमाम ने कहा है कि बी जे पी ने जब ये महसूस कर लिया है कि 25 करोड़ मुसलमानों को नजरअंदाज करके मुल्क को तरक्की की राह पर नहीं ले जाया जा सकता तो हमे इस तब्दीली को महसूस करना चाहिए। इसलिए मैं मुसलमानों से कहता हूँ कि अपनी अक्ल, दानिशमंदी और अपनी समझ से इन नामनिहाद सेकुलर पार्टियों के खोखले वायदों के बजाय गैर-जज्बाती होकर अपने वोटों का इस्तेमाल करें। मुसलमान किसी के बँधवा मजदूर नहीं हैं। वजीर ए आजम ने कहा है कि गुजरात मे जो कुछ हुआ उसे दोहरने नहीं दिया जाएगा। हमें उनके वायदों पर यकीन करना चाहिए।

आप का
सय्यद अहमद बुखारी

Shahi Imam's appeal in support of the BJP

The Shahi Imam of Delhi's Jama Masjid has called upon the Muslims of India to vote for the BJP and pave the way for Mr Atal Bihari Vajpayee to become the Prime Minister of the country again. He argues that the so-called secular political parties have been exploiting Muslims for the last fifty years. They treated Muslims as a vote bank and did nothing for their educational development and/or employment. The Shahi Imam says that the BJP has realized that India cannot move on the path of development by ignoring the presence of the 25 crore Muslims in the country. We must recognize this positive attitude and mindset. I appeal to the Muslims of India to apply their own mind and not get trapped in the shallow promises of the so-called secular parties. Muslims are not the bonded labourers of any political party. The Prime Minister has already assured us that whatsoever happened in Gujarat would not happen again. We must trust him.

Yours
Syed Ahmad Bukhari

A Chronology of Muslim Politics in Postcolonial India

August 1947: On the basis of the Indian Independence Act, 1947, British India was divided into two dominions—India and Pakistan. The princely states were given the choice to either merge with the two dominions or remain independent.

August– September 1947: Massive migration of Muslims from India to Pakistan. Communal riots forced the Muslims of Delhi to take refuge in the big mosques, such as the Jama Masjid.

September 1947: Maulana Abul Kalam Azad organized the All India Azad Muslim Conference to discuss the future role of Muslims in independent India. Many Muslim League leaders joined the Congress.

1948: The Muslim League got divided and the Indian Union Muslim League was established.

1948: Hyderabad state merged with India following police action.

1949: The Constituent Assembly decided to abolish reservation for minorities in legislative bodies and jobs in the final draft of the Constitution.

1950: India and Pakistan signed a treaty known as the Nehru–Liaquat pact for the protection of religious and linguistic minorities.

1951: Azad organized the All India Muslim Convention to appeal to Muslims to give up politics of every kind.

1952: The first general elections successfully took place. Muslims participated enthusiastically in the electoral process. The overall turnout was 44 per cent, but in Muslim-dominated areas, it was more than 60 per cent.

1955: The All India Jamiat Ulama-e-Hind decided to give up politics and asked Muslims to participate in the nation-building project.

1958: Abdul Wahid Owaisi revived the All India Majlis-e-Ittehadul Muslimeen in Hyderabad.

1964: The All India Muslim Majlis-e-Mushawarat, a coalition of various Muslim organizations, was formed as a consultative body.

1965: War with Pakistan.

1967: The Muslim Majlis-e-Mushawarat asked Muslims to vote for a few 'selected' candidates in the Lok Sabha and Assembly elections. The protection of the life and property of Muslims, the protection of Urdu, the minority character of Aligarh Muslim University and non-interference in Muslim personal law emerged as core 'Muslim issues'.

1967: The Congress lost the elections in nine states.

1968: The Enemy Property Act, 1968, was passed by the Parliament. The act empowered the government to regulate the appropriation of property in India owned by those who have taken up Pakistani nationality.

1968: A political party named Muslim Majlis was formed.

1971: War with Pakistan began, followed by a second partition of South Asia, and East Pakistan became Bangladesh

1971: The Congress under Indira Gandhi won the Lok Sabha elections.

1972: The AIMPLB was formed in Mumbai, especially to respond to the debate on the adoption bill.

1974: The imam of Jama Masjid, Abdullah Bukhari, was approached by the Congress. He issued a statement in favour of the government's family planning programme. It was circulated as a fatwa.

1974: Imam Bukhari began to oppose Indira Gandhi. He was arrested under the Maintenance of Internal Security Act, 1971, but later released. He was approached by the Opposition parties.

1975: Emergency was declared.

1976: A Muslim locality was forcibly demolished at Turkman Gate, Delhi. Nineteen people died.

1977: The Janata Party (JP) was formed; Imam Bukhari issued an election fatwa in favour of the JP.

1978: The Minorities Commission was formed by the JP government. The Congress opposed it.

1978: The Second Backward Classes Commission, known as the Mandal Commission, was set up. It proposed a formula to include non-Hindu communities in the OBC category.

1979: Indira Gandhi wrote an open letter to Imam Bukhari requesting him to support the Congress. Bukhari agreed and campaigned for the Congress in the elections.

1980: Indira Gandhi won the Lok Sabha elections.

1980: The Gopal Singh Panel for minorities was constituted.

1983: The Gopal Singh Panel submitted its report. It was never discussed publicly.

1984: The Vishwa Hindu Parishad began its first yatra for the Ram temple. The Congress supported it. The local Muslims of Faizabad formed the Babri Masjid Action Committee, Faizabad. No national Muslim leader showed any interest in this issue.

1984: Indira Gandhi was assassinated. Imam Bukhari supported Rajiv Gandhi in the 1984 elections.

1985: The Supreme Court's verdict was pronounced in the Shah Bano case, favouring maintenance given to an aggrieved divorced Muslim woman.

1985: The AIMPLB launched a nationwide movement against the Supreme Court verdict.

1985: The Rajiv Gandhi government accepted the demands of the conservative ulema led by Ali Mian Nadwi of the Nadwa. It paved the way for the Muslim Women (Protection of Rights on Divorce) Act, 1986, that nullified the Supreme Court judgement.

1986: Babri Masjid, which was occupied by a local mob in 1949, was opened to Hindu worshippers.

1986: The all-India level Babri Masjid Conference was held in Delhi.

1987: The first-ever Muslim political coalition on Babri Masjid, the Babri Masjid Movement Coordination Committee (BMMCC) was formed under the leadership of Syed Shahabuddin.

1988: The Babri Masjid coalition disintegrated into two fractions: the BMMCC led by Shahabuddin and the All India Babri Masjid Action Committee (ABMAC) led by Abdullah Bukhari.

1989: Both fractions supported the Janata Dal (JD) in elections. V.P. Singh formed a non-Congress government with the help of the BJP and the communist parties.

1990: The BJP withdrew their support to the government after the arrest of Advani during his Rath Yatra to Ayodhya.

1990: Chandra Shekhar formed a new government with the help of the Congress. The Shahabuddin group supported the government.

1990: Negotiations between Muslim groups and the VHP began.

1991: The Congress won the elections in the name of secularism and P.V. Narasimha Rao became the prime minister.

1992:　　Babri Masjid was demolished by *kar sevak*s.

1992:　　The first Muslim convention on reservations was held in Delhi.

1993:　　A series of bomb blasts occurred in Bombay (now Mumbai).

1993:　　The National Commission for Minorities (NCM) as a statutory body was established. Muslims were declared a national religious minority. The BJP opposed the NCM.

1993:　　The All India United Muslim Morcha was formed by Dr Ejaz Ali to demand the inclusion of Muslim Dalits in the Scheduled Caste (SC) list.

1998:　　The NDA, led by the BJP, was formed and won the elections. The BJP gave up its core Hindutva issues to sustain the coalition.

1998:　　The All India Pasmanda Muslim Mahaz was formed by Ali Anwar. He demanded that the reservation system be secularized and Dalit Muslims and Dalit Christians be given SC status.

1999:　　The NDA formed the government under Atal Bihari Vajpayee.

2000:　　The BJP-led government reconstituted the National Commission for Minorities.

2002:　　Riots occurred in Gujarat in which around 1000 people, mainly Muslims, were killed.

2004:　　The imam of the Jama Masjid supported the BJP in the elections and asked Muslims to vote for the party. The UPA came to power.

2005: The prime minister's 15 Point Programme was launched.

2006: The Sachar Committee was set up to evaluate Muslim backwardness.

2007: The Sachar Committee submitted its report. The cabinet accepted all the recommendations. The BJP opposed it.

2008: The Ranganath Misra Commission submitted its report. It recommended reservations for Muslims.

2009: The UPA, led by the Congress, won the national elections again.

2013: Riots took place in Muzaffarnagar, western UP.

2014: The BJP-led NDA won the elections. Narendra Modi formed the government.

2015: The first mob-lynching case was reported. It was followed by similar incidents in north India. An aggressive cow-protection movement was launched by pro-BJP groups.

2016: The *'ghar wapsi'* agitation was launched to reconvert Muslims.

2019: The Muslim Women (Protection of Rights on Marriage) Ordinance was passed.

Introduction: Muslims as a Political Question

Do Muslims need purification in 2019?

In a speech dedicated to Deen Dayal Upadhyaya, the founder of the Bharatiya Jana Sangh, Prime Minister Narendra Modi, argued:

> Pandit Upadhyaya used to say no '*ang*' (part) of society is untouchable for us. But many people misunderstand the BJP and project us wrongfully. The definition of secularism in currency is distorted. It runs down the 'desh bhakts' (patriots) . . . Fifty years ago, Pandit Upadhyaya said, 'do not reward/appease (*puraskrit*) Muslims, do not shun (*tiraskrit*) them but purify (*parishkar*) them'. Do not treat Muslims like *vote ki mandi ka maal* (vote banks) or *ghrina ki vastu* (object of hatred). *Unhe apna samjho* (regard them as your own).[1]

Perhaps this was the only occasion when Modi addressed Muslims as a recognizable social group after becoming the prime minister in 2014. Interestingly, however, he did not deviate from fairly popular perceptions about Muslims in India and their role in national politics. Modi raised three rather clichéd metaphors—*Muslim appeasement, the Muslim vote bank* and, the most predictable, *the Indianization of Muslims*—to make them textbook patriots.

These metaphors, no doubt, have acquired a place in our public discussions. Yet, the manner in which the political behaviour of Muslims as a category of analysis has been relegated to the margins in the last four years is rather unprecedented. This book is a modest attempt to unpack the symbols, metaphors and stereotypes associated with Muslims in India and their political inclinations.

There is a strong argument that the rise of the BJP and its Hindutva politics is going to dominate the political discourse in 2019; thus, the conventional 'Muslim politics' of bargain and appeasement is no longer relevant. The political class, the argument goes, is not interested in debating inclusiveness and diversity, primarily because these issues do not work in hardcore interest-based, competitive electoral politics. The increasing social base of the BJP, especially among Dalits and Adivasis, is presented as 'evidence' to show that the 'grand Hindutva unity', which the BJP has always been dreaming of, has finally been achieved.

This argument is presented in two different ways. It is claimed that the 'Modi wave' has destroyed the old caste-based, religion-based vote-bank politics. Therefore, there is no need to address the specific interests of any particular community of voters in elections. In this framework, electoral promises made for any religious/linguistic minority are treated as a deviation from the nationalistic slogan: 'Sabka Saath, Sabka Vikas'.

On the contrary, however, this ultra-developmentalism is also used to underline Hindu subjugation and victimhood. The aggressive campaigns for 'ghar wapsi' and 'love jihad' and the lynching of Muslims in the name of cow worship were seen as 'natural reactions of subjugated Hindus'. In an interview, BJP president, Amit Shah, said:

Development agenda and ghar wapsi have nothing to do with one another. The way of thinking should be changed.

Conversion is a problem [. . .] Not a single so-called secular party has come forward on this. Should forcible conversion be stopped or not? I believe they should be. So those who want to stop forcible conversion should come with us.[2]

This intentional overlapping between development and Hindu victimhood actually began in 2014. The BJP's national slogan 'Sabka Saath, Sabka Vikas', which was presented as a mantra to achieve equality-based citizenship, found a completely different political overtone at local levels.

For example, in UP's Muzaffarnagar district (where a series of communal riots took place in September 2013), the BJP relied heavily on communal polarization. Making an obvious reference to these riots in an election speech, Amit Shah asserted that 'the 2014 Lok Sabha polls were an opportunity to seek revenge for the insult inflicted during the riots in Muzaffarnagar.'[3] Although an FIR was filed against him for using the word 'revenge', the BJP continued to highlight the Muzaffarnagar riots as Hindu subjugation.

Muslim politics, interestingly, is also redefined through the prism of this new configuration of Hindutva politics, that is, 'Development' + 'Sabka Saath, Sabka Vikas' + 'Hindu victimhood'. It is claimed that Muslims are in search of workable survival strategies, which might help them get adjusted to the Modi phenomena. Muslim leaders of the BJP often claim that Muslims must embrace the BJP to create a space for themselves in such a Modi-centric political environment. In a recent article, BJP leader Zafar Islam argues:

The real and pertinent question is: Who is keeping the Muslims out of power? It's the Muslim community which is responsible for making its votes valueless and redundant by becoming a captive vote bank for the Congress and a few other parties, but completely ignoring the BJP which is a ruling party and works in a non-partisan manner.[4]

How to (not) understand Muslim politics?

In my view, this imagination of Muslim politics seems problematic for three reasons. First, the Hindu–Muslim religious–political divide is not the main determining aspect of diversity and pluralism in India. There are a number of different communities which recognize themselves as Hindu or Muslim in a variety of ways. Therefore, translating population data into an electoral majority–minority at the national level is a highly misleading exercise. Muslim communities, like any other social group, participate in electoral politics at the constituency level, responding to a number of regional and local considerations, which do not necessarily relate to the national picture.

Secondly, the distinction between Muslim participation and Muslim representation is very important. The debate on Muslim political representation is all about the decreasing number of Muslim MLAs and MPs. It is assumed that Muslim voters would eventually vote for a Muslim candidate, and that the region, caste, class, gender and party affiliation would not affect their electoral choices. This imaginary correlation between Muslim voters and the elected MLAs and MPs is entirely incorrect. The shrinking presence of Muslim legislators in the assemblies and Parliament does not reflect the nature of Muslim political participation. For instance, there are only twenty-three Muslim MPs in the Lok Sabha at present, which is the lowest Muslim representation in the lower house since 1952 (see Table 1 on p. xliii). However, if we look at the voting percentage of Muslims in the 2014 elections, we might come across a very different picture (see Table 2 on p. xliv). Muslims participated in the electoral process with great eagerness and that has been the reason why the Muslim voting percentage at the national level is remarkably impressive. To understand Muslim politics, therefore, is not merely to analyse the question of Muslim representation—the declining number of MPs and MLAs. The political enthusiasm among the Muslims of India for democracy, their faith in public institutions and their active participation in all forms of politics must also be recognized (see Table 3 and Table 4 on pp. xliv and xlv, respectively).

Finally, there is a difference between so-called media-driven 'Muslim issues' and the everyday anxieties of Muslim communities. For instance, triple talaq is portrayed as the ultimate issue that plagues Muslim women. It is claimed, quite stridently, in fact, that talaq is the most important reason behind the marginalization and under-representation of Muslim women in public life. As expected, a binary between mullahs and progressives has been created and we are left with only two options—yes or no to triple talaq! No one bothered to look at the religious diversity among Muslims, the changing educational and occupational profile of Muslim women at different levels and the nature of contemporary Muslim patriarchy. No rational mind can support triple talaq; but presenting marriage and divorce as decisive political concerns for Muslim communities in general and Muslim women in particular is a highly superficial, distorted and absurd explanation.

What is 'siyasi' about Muslims?

Muslim politics has always been understood in a negative sense. Political descriptions such as 'Muslim communalism', 'Muslim separatism' and, very recently, 'Muslim/Islamic terrorism' are used interchangeably to describe Muslim politics. Although the debates of the early 2000s on social exclusion and inclusion offered official acceptability to the multilayered Muslim under-representation and backwardness in various spheres, Muslim politics continues to be defined in a rather elitist way.

Muslim politics, in this sense, is not about the arguments, statements and claims made by Muslim leaders and religious elites. These Muslim political stakeholders, no doubt, do have an intrinsic relationship with Muslim communities. But the political vocabulary they use to argue on behalf of Muslim communities always comes from competitive electoral politics. For instance, when a Muslim leader of the BJP says: 'Muslims have a message for their counterparts . . . BJP is not communal but painted so systematically . . . Give them a fair chance. . . .'[5] he actually implies that Muslims are not going to vote for Modi and the only solution is that they must vote for him!

The challenge, therefore, is not merely to analyse the question of Muslim representation—the declining number of MPs, MLAs—but to go beyond this neat and clear portrayal of Muslim politics. That is what this book explores. Instead of offering a grand narrative of political Islam/Muslims in the Indian subcontinent, it identifies two broad questions:

- What are the sociocultural sources which contribute to the Muslim political identity in contemporary India?
- Do the Muslims of India constitute a political community?

This book does not aim at *defining* Muslim politics in India. Instead, it looks at the ways in which Muslim politics as a template is used to describe statements, actions and processes. In other words, the book studies Muslim politics as a political discourse—an intellectual mode through which certain specific notions of Muslim identity in contemporary India are produced and sustained.

The term 'siyasi'—an Urdu/Persian word that generally means 'political'—is employed here intentionally to describe the diverse forms of Muslim identity. Two specific justifications might be given in this regard.

First, Muslims are often described as a politically conscious community. The discussion on Muslim vote bank and Muslim appeasement relies on the assumption that Muslims are fully aware of the complexities of the electoral system and therefore always act accordingly. This popular portrayal envisages Muslims as a deeply political community. There is a need to unpack these popular perceptions and, for that reason, *Siyasi Muslims* is conceptually very useful and instructive.

Secondly, there is another meaning to the term 'siyasi'. It is used to denote those individuals and groups who are not trustworthy, who work only to further their own vested interests and never join in with mainstream national interests. The Muslims of India are often defined in these terms. It is alleged that they are obsessed with Islam, which does not allow them to embrace any other identity wholeheartedly. This is the reason we are often told, rightly or wrongly, that they do not sing 'Vande Mataram', that they eat cow meat and support Pakistan. In other words, they are siyasi![6]

These two meanings of the term 'siyasi Muslims' contribute to a very popular yet stereotyped perception of Muslims of India—as an informed and conscious group of people who are untrustworthy and disloyal to the nation!

The book is divided into three parts: (i) Making Sense of Siyasi Muslims, (ii) Unpacking Siyasi Muslims and, finally, (iii) The Politics of Siyasi Muslims.

The first part of the book has four chapters. The first chapter titled 'Muslims, We Know as Numbers' traces the story of the census that transformed Muslims into a numerical entity. It also identifies the paradoxes of modern Indian Muslim identity and tries to answer a very basic question—how to address the highly diversified Indian Muslim community in intellectual terms?

This is followed by a chapter on contemporary Islamic religiosity, 'Muslims as a Religious Community'. Investigating the assumption that Muslims are more religious than other communities, this chapter demonstrates Muslim views on religion and religiosity. These themes are further unpacked in the third chapter, '"Islamization" since Independence', which traces the story of postcolonial Islam as a diversified phenomenon. Discussing the notion of 'Dawat-e-Islam'—inviting Muslims as well as non-Muslims to embrace Islam—the chapter argues that the story of postcolonial Indian Islam cannot be understood without making sense of the debate on Indian secularism. The next chapter, 'Why Does Hindutva Need Muslims', makes an attempt to understand the historically constituted anti-Muslim rhetoric of different forms of Hindutva. It also underlines the genealogy of a few questions that are asked to evaluate the loyalty and patriotism of Muslims.

The second part of the book unravels the structure of the concept of Siyasi Muslims. The fifth chapter, 'Muslims as a Minority', looks at the legal–constitutional technicalities to understand the much talked about status of Muslims as an official minority. It is argued that the minority status of Muslims is not always determined in constitutional terms; instead, it is a product of competitive electoral politics.

The next three chapters are devoted to the internal power structure of the Muslim community. Chapter 6 takes us to the question of Muslim backwardness, especially with regard to the debate on caste-based reservation. Examining various political positions and arguments, the chapter traces the multilayered nature of the Muslim politics of backwardness.

The next chapter, 'The Politics of Triple Talaq', pays close attention to the triple talaq debate. Instead of suggesting what Muslim men do, the chapter looks at the complex argument made by the Muslim women's groups. In the next chapter titled

'The New Muslim Elite', a serious attempt is made to reveal the class structure among Muslims in India. Using the official data of the Government of India and seminal works on Muslim classes, the chapter offers a contemporary conceptualization of the idea of the Muslim elite.

The last part of the book recapitulates these discussions and brings us back to more apparent political questions. The chapter titled 'The Metaphors of Muslim Politics' examines the postcolonial story of the Muslim vote bank. It argues that metaphors of Muslim politics should not be treated as reasoned statements on the objective conditions of Muslims; rather, they must be seen as weapons of electoral politics. The final chapter offers a set of arguments responding to the possible role of Muslims in shaping the future of India's democracy.

A note on sources

The book relies on five types of research material. Official documents, such as parliamentary debates, census reports and election reports published by the Election Commission of India, are the first kind of sources. These documents are used to extract relevant information/data to offer an informed, evidence-based narrative.

The research material—pamphlets, short books in various languages and rare photographs—which I have been collecting for over a decade during the course of my fieldwork in different parts of India is the second major source of information. These ethnographic details provide thick background descriptions to situate the main arguments of the study.

I believe that interviews with religious leaders and Muslim politicians provide relevant first-hand information on critical issues concerning Muslims. Such interviews also introduce us to different perspectives and positions. This is the reason why interviews are considered an important source, especially to make sense of the internal debates among the Muslim elite.

The fourth kind of sources may be referred to as 'online' sources. The websites of leading Muslim religious and political organizations, online newspaper reports and articles are very relevant in understanding public perceptions and debates about contemporary Muslim politics. This is what I have tried to capture in this book.

The data generated by the CSDS-Lokniti on various aspects of Muslim social and political life in post–1947 India is my fifth major source. I have used the National Election Study (NES) data sets for offering a comparative analysis of Muslim politics. *The Religious Attitudes and Behaviours Survey 2015*, which was designed primarily to make sense of the contemporary forms of religiosity, is used extensively to produce research-based arguments on Muslim political identity.

Finally, it is important to make two clarifications here. First, the book does not claim to offer final and conclusive answers to questions posed in the public sphere about Muslims. Rather, it is in an attempt to clarify the nature of public debates and the political reception of such discussions. In this sense, it is a context-driven exploratory exercise. Second, the book is not written to defend the loyalty and nationalism of Muslims in India. As a researcher, I do not claim to represent any Muslim community or group. Nor do I believe in advising the right kind of politics to Muslims. The book is simply an outcome of my engagement with Muslim communities in India as a 'participant observer'.

Table 1: Muslim representation in the Lok Sabha, 1952–2014

No.	Year	Total elected members	No. of elected Muslim members
1	1952	489	21
2	1957	494	24
3	1962	494	23
4	1967	520	29
5	1971	518	30
6	1977	542	34**
7	1980	529*1	49**
8	1984	542	46**
9	1989	529*2	33
10	1991	534*3	28
11	1996	543	28
12	1998	543	29
13	1999	543	32
14	2004	543	36
15	2009	543	30
16	2014	543	23

Notes:

The Muslim members of the Lok Sabha are identified by names. The author has to rely on this method as there is no official source available to get information about the religion espoused by an elected MP.

*1: Elections were not held in Assam (12) and Meghalaya (1)
*2: Elections were not held in Assam (14)
*3: Elections were not held in J&K (6) and countermanded in two seats in Bihar and one in UP
** Including Muslims elected in by-elections

Source: Based on the statistics provided by the Election Commission of India on its official website: https://eci.gov.in/statistical-report/statistical-reports/.

Table 2: Voting percentage compared religion-wise

Religion	2009	2014
Hindus	58	68
Muslims	59	59
Christians	64	69
Sikhs	66	55
Other religions	49	60
TOTAL	58	66

Source: NES 2009, NES 2014, CSDS-Lokniti
Figures in percentages

Table 3: Do Muslims trust public institutions?

Social group	*General trust in public institutions
Hindu Upper Caste	64
OBC	64
SC	60
ST	63
Muslims	63
Others	61

Source: CSDS-Lokniti report, *Democracy in India: A Citizens Perspective* (2015)
Figures in percentages
* 'General trust' has been calculated by adding the responses to nine trust-based questions, such as trust in national government, provincial government, local government, civil services, police, courts, army, Parliament and political parties.

Table 4: How do Muslims participate in politics?

Social group	Persuaded others to vote	Took part in a rally	Signed a petition	Took part in a demonstration
Hindu Upper Caste	18	22	30	22
OBC	20	21	31	28
SC	14	20	24	20
ST	15	16	26	19
Muslims	22	23	26	28
Others	9	13	19	15

Source: CSDS-Lokniti report, *Democracy in India: A Citizens Perspective* (2015)

Figures are in percentages and based on a series of questions

PART I

MAKING SENSE OF SIYASI MUSLIMS

1

Muslims, We Know as 'Numbers'!

Many people . . . object to Hindus flaunting saffron robes and trishuls at rallies. While a burkha may not be a weapon, in a symbolic sense it is akin to a trishul. It represents the most reactionary, antediluvian aspects of the faith. To object to its display in public is a mark not of intolerance.[1]

Muslims [. . .] once ruled over great kingdoms in Iran, Iraq, Andalusia and Turkey, and indeed in India as well. This political overlordship is long gone; yet, in gorgeous buildings and traditions of music and literature, its traces remain. Facing discrimination in the present, many Muslims seek consolation in a return to the past, by thinking, acting and dressing in a form they believe is consistent with the Golden Age their community is said to have once enjoyed.[2]

Ramachandra Guha made these comments in his articles responding to a debate on Muslimness in contemporary India. As a public intellectual, Guha's critique of Hindutva is well known. He has been arguing for the protection of rights of all marginalized sections of Indian society, including Muslims. Hence, it would be absolutely incorrect to brand Guha as an anti-Muslim intellectual.

3

These comments, however, are not merely indicative of Guha's provocative mode of argumentation. No doubt, his intention is to provoke his liberal adversaries to look at Muslims not only as victims but also as a ghettoized, backward-looking socio-religious group. But the manner in which he makes these comments also introduces us to Guha's reliability on popular perceptions about Muslims. He, too, like others, uses three popular beliefs—Muslims as a single pan-Islamic community, the burkha as an icon of Muslim women's subjugation and the nostalgia of the royal Islamic past—to underline the internal problems of the Muslims of India.

Although Guha was severely criticized for his remarks on the burkha and Muslim backwardness by a number of authors and activists, his imagination of Muslims as a homogeneous community was not scrutinized adequately. That was the reason why despite being apologetic for his initial generalizations about the symbols of Muslimness, Guha continues to rely on the assumption that there is only one Indian Muslim society in which the burkha is the only universally acceptable Islamic attire for women. He writes:

My comparison was ill-chosen, and the chastisement I received for it is merited. I also agree that the headscarf and the skull-cap are akin to the turban and the vibhooti, markers of religious identity that should not offend anyone when displayed in public. That said, I agree entirely with Ambedkar that the burkha is a mark of suppression, of women from men, and also of separation, of Muslims from non-Muslims. If you hide your face from me, how can we be partners in a shared political project? [. . .] There is unquestionably a need for more progressive leadership among Indian Muslims.[3]

Guha justifies his position by evoking a text Ambedkar wrote in the 1940s! It simply means that he thinks nothing has changed in the last seventy years in Muslim societies. And it is largely due to this reason, perhaps, that it may be legitimate to suggest that Muslims need progressive leaders to avail of citizenship rights!

The question therefore is: How to (and how not to) describe the Muslims of India? This is exactly what this chapter tries to do. It problematizes the numerical representation of the Muslim community as a homogeneous entity and traces the story of Muslims as numbers!

Muslims as numbers: depiction and debates

Being a census category—a category that is employed to count people on various bases, including religion—Muslims are predominately addressed as 'numbers' to describe the demographic configuration of the country. However, unlike other religious communities, Muslims as numbers are always portrayed as an unsolvable national problem. Three different yet connected arguments are often given in this regard.

First of all, there is a popular development-centric argument. It is suggested that the unrestricted growth of the Muslim population affects the equitable and just distribution of national resources in a developing economy like India. This argument relies heavily on the growth rate of the Muslim population—a statistical tool to measure the comparable increase of population in percentage points. Traces of this explanation could easily be found in newspaper reports and prime-time TV discussions.

The English newspapers' headlines of 25 August 2015—the very next day when the government released the latest census statistics on religious communities—is a good example. (See Box 1 on the following page.) It demonstrates how the metaphor of Muslims as numbers is used in public discourse. Being the most accessible form of information about Muslims in India, the population in percentages (Muslims constitute 14.22 per cent of India's total population, and their growth rate is 24.60 per cent, which is higher than that of Hindus!) actually becomes a powerful symbol of Muslim identity.

Box 1: English newspapers' headlines: 25 August 2015

- *'Census 2011: Hindus dip to below 80 per cent of population; Muslim share up, slows down*: The Muslim community has registered a moderate 0.8 per cent growth to touch 17.22 crore in the 10-year period between 2001 and 2011, up from 13.8 crore, while the Hindu population showed a decline by 0.7 per cent at 96.63 crore during the period, the census data said.'[4]
- *'Census 2011 shows Islam is the fastest growing religion in India*: The proportion of Hindus, Sikhs, Buddhists shrank, while there was negligible change for Christians and Jains, shows data.'[5]
- *'Bengal beats India in Muslim growth rate'*[6]

Muslims as numbers is also used as an explanatory framework to understand the relationship between Islamic faith and population growth. It is argued that Muslims are more religious than other religious communities. This faith (read blind faith!) in pre-modern Islamic scriptures, such as the Quran and Hadith, does not allow them to accept the challenges of modern life. As a result, the argument goes, an inward-looking Islamic culture evolves, which discourages Muslim men from adopting family planning. To get rid of this old Islamist mindset, Muslims are advised to embrace modern education in the true sense of the term so that they can understand the significance of birth control. This stereotypical conclusion is often rejected by the professional demographers on the basis of factual inaccuracy.[7] Yet, the belief that the Islamic doctrine is responsible for the Muslim growth rate seems to dominate public imagination.

The third argument is purely political. A section of intellectuals and political elite associated with Hindu nationalist politics invokes separatist tendencies inherent in the Islamic doctrine to argue that Muslim population growth is an outcome of a planned strategy, a deep-rooted conspiracy to outnumber Hindus. These scholars are described as 'saffron demographers'—partly because of their visible anti-Muslim attitude and partly due to their adherence to Hindutva politics.[8] The Partition is referred to as a historical metaphor in these explanations to draw a simple conclusion: a stringent law to control Muslim population must be implemented. The resolution passed by the RSS in November 2015 illustrates this more sharply:

The share of population of religions of Bharatiya origin, which was 88 per cent, has come down to 83.8 per cent, while the Muslim population, which was 9.8 per cent, has increased to 14.23 per cent during the period 1951–2011 [. . .] The rate of growth of Muslim population has been higher than the national average in the border districts of border states like Assam, West Bengal and Bihar, clearly indicating the unabated infiltration from Bangladesh.[9]

These arguments, nevertheless, are critically evaluated on the basis of facts and statistics. The growth rate of the Muslim population is compared with other factors such as median age, average fertility and infant mortality rate by professional demographers and sociologists to produce a nuanced and informed counter-reading. Abusaleh Shariff's thoughtful rejoinder is relevant here. Questioning the 'ready-to-use political conclusion', Shariff argues:

Muslim population has increased from 13.4 per cent of the population to 14.2 per cent, which is 0.8 percentage points higher. But the rate of growth is considerably lower than in previous decades. Muslims are expected to grow faster than Hindus for a couple of more decades because they have the youngest median age and relatively high fertility among the major religious groups in India. In 2010, the median age of Indian Muslims was 22, compared with 26 for Hindus and 28 for Christians. Muslim women bear an average 3.1 children per head, compared with 2.7 for Hindus and 2.3 for Christians.[10]

This counter-reading has an intellectual political relevance of its own, especially in the present apparent anti-Muslim context. It offers us intellectually sophisticated arguments to reject the claims of Hindutva-inspired saffron demography—a set of pernicious myths about claimed differences between the Hindu and Muslim population, which has somehow become part of our 'common wisdom'.[11] The hollowness of the popular discourse on Muslim population, which is systematically used by the political class for its own vested interests, is also exposed in these writings.

However, this informed critique of stereotypical imaginations of the Muslim population survives primarily in academic discussions and seminars. It does not affect the popular belief that 'the Muslim population is a threat' to the nation. Even the so-called secular political parties do not show any interest in evolving an alternative political position on Muslims as numbers. The question is—why?

Let us take an example to elaborate this point. Table 1 on the following page gives us an overview of the Hindu and Muslim populations in India since 1881. The table is based on data collected from different official sources. A very broad overview of the table may suggest that the Muslim population has been constantly increasing since the late nineteenth century and that the decadal growth rate of Muslims is always higher than Hindus. On the basis of this set of information, it is quite possible to look at the following probabilities: Muslims have more wives; they produce more children; the Quran permits them to increase population; and, if this trend continues, Muslims are certainly going to outnumber Hindus!

The social scientists—professional demographers, sociologists and historians—might not like to look at this table in this way.

They could argue that the data presented in the table is not self-explanatory and that one should read these aggregate numbers with other variables (such as region, language, gender and literacy level, etc.) in order to grasp the nuanced demographic picture presented in the table. This expert view, no doubt, encourages us to make a distinction between *data* and the *meanings/interpretations* of data. However, these kinds of overtly academic responses do not help us in unpacking the ways in which popular beliefs and stereotypes are justified by using 'scientific facts'.

This is precisely the reason why we must focus on the historical making of popular imaginations. In my view, therefore, a genealogy of Muslims as numbers in modern India must be traced.

Table 1: Population of India, 1881–2011

Year	Hindus	Muslims	Hindus %	Muslims %	Hindu growth rate	Muslim growth rate
1881	187.8	49.9	75.1	20		
1891	207.6	57.1	74.2	20.4	10.5	14.4
1901	206.9	62.1	72.9	21.9	-0.3	8.8
1911	217.2	67.8	71.7	22.4	5.0	9.2
1921	216.2	71.0	70.7	23.2	-0.4	4.7
1931	238.6	79.3	70.7	23.5	10.3	11.7
1941	270.2	94.4	69.4	24.3	13.2	19.0
1951	303.6	35.4	84.9	9.9		
1961	366.5	46.9	83.4	10.7	20.7	32.5
1971	453.4	61.4	82.7	11.2	23.7	30.9
1981	549.7	75.7	82.6	11.4	24.4	30.9
1991	687.6	101.6	82.0	12.1	22.8	32.8
2001	827.5	138.1	80.5	13.4	19.92	29.52
2011	966.3	172.2	79.8	14.23	16.7	24.6

Source: Compiled by the author on the basis of the various census reports of India.
Figures in millions

Muslims as numbers: A story!

The story of Muslims as numbers should begin from colonial India. The imperial regime—the East India Company as well as the British state of India—relied heavily on its knowledge-producing techniques (the census, organization of land records, research on religion, culture and history of the native population, etc.) to administer the empire. Although it would be incorrect to describe this British quest for knowledge merely as a reflection of the 'divide and rule policy' in direct political terms, the significant role of colonial knowledge in producing a new language of politics in India cannot entirely be ruled out.

The colonial census produced statistical data with regard to Indian social groups. In this process, religious groups such as Hindus, Muslims, Christians, Sikhs and Parsis were converted into 'populations'. The numerically superior data set came to be known as 'majority', while numerically inferior data set turned out to be a 'minority', i.e., Hindus as a majority and non-Hindus (mainly Muslims and Sikhs) as minorities. Let us take three examples to understand the ways in which Muslims were conceived as numbers.

John Strachey's famous textbook *India* (1894), in which he categorically argues that India cannot be understood as a nation, is my first example. He writes:

India is a name which we give to a great region including a multitude of different countries. There is no general Indian term that corresponds [to] it [. . .] This is the first and most essential thing to learn about India—that there is not, and never was an India or even any country of India, possessing, according to European ideas, any sort of unity, physical, political, social or religious; no Indian nation, and especially no 'people of India', of which we hear so much.[12]

Strachey thinks that British rule is necessary for this land because it could provide an administrative unity to the social and religious diversity of Indian people. His description of the Muslims of India is very instructive. According to him, the Muslims of this land are not entirely Islamic as 'they are ignorant of the religion to which they nominally belong, and so little devoted to its tenets, that they might almost as properly be counted among the innumerable classes of Hindus'.[13] However, in order to classify Muslims into one measurable category, he makes an interesting distinction between the Muslims of foreign origin and Muslim converts. He writes:

The dominant races of Pathans and Baluchis are of foreign origin, but the majority of the population consists of the descendants of Hindus or aboriginal tribes, who long accepted, more or less, the religion of their conquerors.[14]

We have now two kinds of Muslims: the foreigners, the warriors and those who won India; and the local Muslims who were converted to Islam long ago but who are not fully Islamic. The foreigners, Strachey notes, 'hold a more influential position in the country than their mere numbers would give them; they are [. . .] energetic than Hindus, and possess greater independence of character. In perfection of manner and courtesy a Mohammedan gentleman of northern India has often no superior'.[15] The distinction between India's Muslims and the ruling tribes of Muslims, Strachey argues, evaporates in the nineteenth century when the movements to 'purify Islamic faith' among Muslims begins. In his opinion, 'the more orthodox a Mohammedan becomes, the wider becomes the gulf that separates him from every form of idolatrous worship'.[16] Strachey expects that purification of Islam would not merely produce a homogeneous Muslim community but would also empower them to imbibe the courage and determination of the ruling classes. This description very clearly tells us how a category called Muslims is produced and legitimated.

The census report of 1891 is the second example. This report makes another very crucial and powerful observation about Muslims by establishing a direct link between the Muslim population of British India and the Muslims in the world. It notes: 'The Musalman population of the world has been roughly estimated at various amounts from 70 to 90 millions, so that whatever the real figure may be between those limits, the Indian Empire contains a large majority of the followers of the Prophet.'[17] The report also makes a comparison between Hindu and Muslim population growth, probably for the first time in India. It argues:

As regards the progress of the faith of Islam [. . .] it has been undoubtedly rapid in Eastern Bengal, and has been perceptible, though on somewhat an uncertain basis, in the Punjab. Elsewhere, the increase seems to be mostly that due to normal growth. But so far as regards the large and heterogeneous class of urban Musalmans found all over the country, it is possible that that growth may have been actually impeded by the difficulty found in getting a living under the new conditions of British rule. For the minimum of literary instruction required now as a passport to even the lower grades of middle-class public employ is decidedly higher than it used to be, whilst the progress of learning amongst this class of Musalmans has not proportionately advanced, and with the comparatively small number of recruits for the army, police and menial offices that is now found sufficient, few outlets remain available. It is possible that some such reason as this accounts for the fact that the general rate of increase outside the tracts above mentioned is a little below that found to prevail amongst the population as a whole.[18]

Envisaging Indian Muslims as an inseparable part of a pan-Islamic community, the census report interprets the growth of Muslims in British India as 'spread of Islam'. The lack of education among Muslims and their limited participation in public life are seen as some of the other specific reasons behind population growth. The expectation that educational empowerment would enlighten Muslims to embrace modernity is clearly reflected here. If this official expectation is reread with regard to John Strachey's observation that Muslims were going to become more Islamic in the near future, the genesis of a very powerful thesis in favour of Muslim separatism could easily be traced. It is now possible to imagine the religious reforms (Islamization!) among Muslims as an assertion of their exclusive Muslimness. This Muslimness, as an unadulterated and pure Islamic identity, was invariably presented in opposition to authentic Hindu/Indian distinctiveness. 'Muslims as numbers' emerges as a powerful tool to substantiate this official reading of late nineteenth-century Indian society.

This straightforward classification of Indian religious groups as populations also functioned differently at another level. By the early nineteenth century, colonial historical researchers produced an equally powerful discourse of authentic India. The Hindus were seen as the old, natural and authentic habitants of this land (although Aryan invasion theory later complicated this kind of reasoning!) as all their revered places of worship were situated in the geopolitical entity called the Indian subcontinent. The Muslims, the numerically second-most powerful group, who were also the rulers of this land before the British, were considered to be the outsiders. James Mill, the British political historian—who wrote the famous book *The History of British India* in 1823—is a revealing example to underline this colonial thesis.

It is worth noting that Mill—who never visited India—was the first official British historian who divided Indian history into three periods: the Hindu, the Muslim and the British. Mill identifies only two sets of people in India: Hindus and Muslims. In his opinion, the original inhabitants of this land of India were the Hindus, who had always been backward by European standards. Muslims, on the other hand, as per Mill, were superior to Hindus in all respects. That was the reason why, Mill argued, Muslims were able to rule over Hindus. The British, in this sequence, were superior to Muslims and, hence, were the natural rulers of India. He writes:

> At the time when the nations of Europe opened their communication with India, by the Cape of Good Hope, the people whom we have now described had for a number of ages been subject to a race of foreigners. That subjection, though it had not greatly altered the texture of native society, had introduced new forms into some of the principal departments of state; had given the military command to foreigners; and had mixed with the population a proportion of a people differing from them considerably, in manners, character, and religion. The political state of India, at this time, consisted of a Mahomedan government, supported by a Mahomedan force, over a Hindu population.[19]

The scope of this 'authentic India theory' was further expanded to answer a few empirically complicated questions. For instance, why did Hindus as a collectivity fail to protect their land despite being a majority in medieval India?

The existence of caste was projected as one of the main reasons behind Hindu subjugation. It was asserted that since Hindu society was not united on caste lines, it could not resist the powerful Muslim invasion that changed the course of Indian history. According to Mill:

> Mahomedans were exempt from the institution of caste; that institution which stands a more effectual barrier against the

welfare of human nature than any other institution which the workings of caprice and of selfishness have ever produced. Under the Mahomedan despotisms of the East, nearly as much as in republics themselves, all men are treated as equal. There is no noble, no privileged class.[20]

Mill does not stop here. He goes on to describe the temperament and mannerisms of Hindus and Muslims. He writes:

In point of address and temper, the Mahomedan is less soft, less smooth and winning than the Hindu. Of course he is not so well liked by his lord and master the Englishman, who desires to have nothing more to do with him, than to receive his obedience. In truth, the Hindu, like the eunuch, excels in the qualities of a slave. The indolence, the security, the pride of the despot, political or domestic, [they] find less to hurt them in the obedience of the Hindu, than in that of almost any other portion of the species. But if less soft, the Mahomedan is more manly, more vigorous. He more nearly resembles our own half-civilized ancestors; who, though more rough, were not more gross; though less supple in behaviour, were still more susceptible of increased civilization, than a people in the state of the Hindus.[21]

This *masculine* representation of all Muslims fits well with two corresponding Muslim images: the image of a temple destroyer and the image of a bully! Hence, the claim, that Muslims, despite being less in numbers, looted and desecrated the Hindu temples and transformed them into mosques and also dishonoured Hindu women and forced them to convert to Islam, was legitimized. This overtly historical explanation found a powerful 'scientific' justification in the late nineteenth century when census data began to acquire the status of uncontested rational knowledge.

This colonial imagination of Muslims as numbers also offered a new kind of self-perception to Muslim communities. It now became possible for them to think of a homogeneous pan-Islamic Muslim community, the exact numbers of its members, its history, its authentic religion and, above all, its common political interests as a group. This self-perception encouraged the religious elites of the nineteenth century to search for the authentic Islam, which in effect led to religious reform movements. At the same time, the realization or recognition that there could be collective (read communal) interests paved the way for the debates on political representation.

Muslims as numbers: Representation without voting rights!

It is important to note here that the debates on communal/community representation are intractably linked to another powerful debate—the inclusion of Indians in the British political system. The representation of Indians at various levels of administration was first introduced by the Council Act of 1861, which was later expanded in 1892. But the inclusion of natives in 'responsible government' was contingent upon another equally puzzling question: who would or could legitimately be called the 'Indian representative'? By this time, Hindus and Muslims had become two separate groups as well as two distinct political entities in the British imagination. And, by this logic, there was no possibility of having a British-style representative government in India. In other words, Hindus and Muslims being the *permanent* majority and minority, respectively, was not suitable for the rationale of representative government at all.

Two popular British arguments are relevant here. First, common Indians did not have 'individual rationality'; hence, they were not mature enough to run an individual voter-centric modern democracy; and second, India as a political entity was highly diversified; therefore, it could not become a European-style 'nationality', nor, for that matter, a nation state. In this sense, both Hindus and Muslims as Indians are unfit for democracy; and even if they are given some democratic space in responsible government, they are certainly not going to utilize it because of their inherent hostility towards each other.[22] However, it does not mean that there were no possibilities to prepare Indian communities for active national politics. In the first decade of the twentieth century, the colonial state devised an interesting mechanism to accommodate Indians in legislative bodies.

The British legislative structures were designed in such a way that the interests of various competing groups could be addressed. The introduction of separate electorates for Muslims in 1909 was one such move. The Government of India acts of 1919 and 1935 extended these provisions to Sikhs, Indian Christians and a host of other communal and occupational groups. In 1925, the colonial government initiated the policy of reserving a certain percentage of direct appointments to government service for Muslims. This was further extended to other communities under the Government of India Act of 1935.

The separate electorate does not mean that all Muslims, who were recognized as numbers by the British, would have a voting right to elect a Muslim representative. Actually, it was the outcome of a struggle between the Hindu and Muslim elite. We must remember that in the post-1857 period, a strong pro-British Muslim politics evolved, especially after the formation of the Aligarh school in 1875 by Syed Ahmad Khan. The Aligarh school consolidated the position of an emerging class of an English-educated, upper-caste, upper-class Muslim elite, who found it difficult to compete with the English-educated and already established Hindu (especially Bengali) elite. This competition became very obvious in the 1890s when the question of representation of Indians in councils and other bodies came up after the enactment of the Council Act.

The Muslim elite made two points. First, in all elections (legislative councils or for local bodies) the Muslims must be represented by Muslims, and these Muslim representatives must separately be elected by purely Muslim voters. Secondly, and perhaps most importantly, it was argued that the Muslim community's representation must be commensurate not merely with their numerical strength but also with their political importance and the value of the contribution they make to the defence of the empire.[23] These two demands became the basis for an important colonial technique—the weightage system. The Muslims (read Muslim elite!) were given more seats than they were entitled to by numbers only, and, even while voting in general constituencies side by side with Hindus, they were required to vote for their own members in separate and wholly Muslim constituencies.[24]

In other words, under the 1909 act, Muslim voters were given the following rights:

1. The right to elect their representatives
2. The right to elect their representatives by separate electorates
3. The right to vote in the general electorates as well
4. The right to weightage in representation[25]

But who were these *Muslim voters* in British India?

It is worthwhile to remember that the colonial state did not expand the scope of voting rights. In the Government of India Act of 1919, for instance, the elected constituencies were classified into general constituencies and special constituencies. The general constituents were further divided into Muhammadan, non-Muhammadan, European, non-European and Sikh constituencies. Interestingly, except religion, the qualifications for being a voter in all general constituencies remained the same. The 'ownership or occupation of a building, assessment to or payment of municipal or cantonment of rates or taxes, assessment to or payment of income tax and the holding of land' were the criteria to identify a male member of a community as a voter. It simply means that the majority of Muslims, who did not have land, who were not taxpayers, and were poor and marginalized, did not have any right to vote!

The *Indian Franchise Committee Report* of 1932, which was set up to map out the debate on popular elections and universal adult franchise, very categorically argued:

> In agreement with all local Governments and provincial Committees, the Committee are of opinion that [. . .] the introduction of complete adult franchise is impracticable in India [. . .] The Committee recommend that the franchise in all the provinces should be based on the following qualifications:
>
> > (a) Property [. . .] which has been the basis for the franchise hitherto, should be retained as one qualification for the vote;
> > (b) Education [. . .] an educational qualification should be introduced which will be independent of property, and which should, so far as possible, be uniform throughout the country.[26]

It shows that the British state was hesitant to recognize the idea of popular democracy in India. However, at the same time, it showed great interest in addressing the Hindus and Muslims as numbers. This paradoxical equation—representation with democracy—continued to dominate the political discourse in the 1940s. The weightage system was understood either as a reflection of Muslim appeasement or as a recognition of the political distinctness of the Muslims of India as a nation. These debates of high politics, quite astonishingly, did not pay attention to the fact that only rich, educated and propertied Hindus and Muslims were entitled to elect the Muslim/Hindu elites as their representatives!

Muslims as numbers: Minority, nationality or second majority?

Two corresponding developments—the evolution of the British judicial system in India and the emergence of religious reform movements of the nineteenth century—also helped in consolidating the Muslims as numbers in a significant way. The colonial state recognized the religiously sanctioned norms and customs of each religious community on the lines of the prevalent notion of the customary law. The policy of non-intervention, which the British strictly adhered to, paved the way for a new category of laws and 'personal laws'. The Shariat Application Act, 1937, is very relevant in elaborating this point.

The term 'sharia' or 'shariat', which became a dominant idiom of Muslim religiosity in colonial/postcolonial India, was legally defined as a collection of codified rules and norms based on the Quran and Hadiths (the sayings and acts of Prophet Muhammad). Since this codification has always been subject to various interpretations, there were various shariats among Sunnis and Shias. However, the idea that the shariat should be treated as the most authentic set of governing principles for Indo-Islamic communities came into existence only in the eighteenth century. Despite the fact that a large part of the subcontinent was ruled by Muslim kings and rulers before the British, the norms to govern political affairs as well as the sociocultural life of Muslims were not entirely based on a set of rules and interpretations called the shariat. There were many different sources which constituted the religious beliefs and practices of various Islamic communities. These historically evolved religious–cultural practices were termed 'customary laws', which were separated from 'personal' laws in the later period by the British judiciary.

The translation of the Quran (in Persian and later in Urdu) and circulation of the *Tafseer* (explanation of the Quran) literature the established a clear distinction between shariat-based ideal Islam and the customary practices associated with various Muslim communities in the mid-nineteenth century. The Muslim reformers, particularly the ulema, constructed a highly idealized picture of classical Islam and started marking the actual cultural practices as un-Islamic. In fact, the term 'gair sharia' (anti-shariat) was established as an explanatory category in religious texts. Since shariat-based Islam had already been recognized by the colonial state, following its policy of non-intervention, customary practices lost their potential as a source of law. The Mussalman Wakf Validating Act, 1913, and the Muslim Personal Law (Shariat) Application Act, 1937, in this sense, were evolved out of this legal schema.

The representation of 'personal law' as the most authentic and legally sanctioned and codified form of Islamic customs was used very intelligently by the Muslim political elite. In September 1937, for example, M.A. Jinnah proposed to make it compulsory for all Indian Muslims to be governed by shariat law. The Muslim leaders of the Congress also used this legally sanctioned shariat law to show Muslim distinctiveness. They conceptualized shariat law as a sacred doctrine, which could not be amended or changed, and precisely for this reason it had to be protected to ensure the religious rights of Muslims in the proposed constitutional framework. The religious bond constituted by the shariat actually turned out to be a reference point for asserting Muslim political oneness in a strictly numerical sense.

Two powerful political speeches made in 1940 are relevant in elaborating this point.

Maulana Abul Kalam Azad, the Congress president, in his 1940 presidential address at Ramgarh, said:

The Muslims in India number between 80–90 million. The same types of social or racial divisions, which affect other communities, do not divide them. The powerful bonds of Islamic brotherhood and equality have protected them to a large extent from the weakness that flows from social divisions. It is true that they number only one-fourth of the total population; but the question is not one of the population ratio, but of the large numbers and the strength behind them. Can such a vast mass of humanity have any legitimate reason for apprehension that in a free and democratic India, it might be unable to protect its rights and interests?[27]

M.A. Jinnah, the Quaid-e-Azam (great leader) of the Muslim League, also made very similar remarks in his presidential address at Lahore in 1940. He said:

Musalman are not a minority, as it is commonly known and understood. One has got to look around. Even today, according to the British map of India, 4 out of 11 provinces, where Muslims dominate more or less, are functioning notwithstanding the decision of the Hindu Congress High Command to non-cooperate and prepare for civil disobedience. Musalmans are a nation according to any definition of a nation, and they must have their homeland, their territory and their state.[28]

Both Jinnah and Azad, despite taking two very different positions, seemed to adhere to the claim that Muslims should be recognized as a powerful numerical entity. For Azad, the protection of Muslim distinctiveness is only possible in a secular, united India because secular nationalism ensures the rights of religious minorities. However, for Jinnah, the Muslim right to self-determination is just and legitimate because Muslims as a community constitute a nation in the modern sense. Interestingly, both the arguments survived: India was partitioned and the Muslims of Pakistan eventually became a nationality; and a large number of Muslims remained in India as the largest religious minority. In fact, that was the reason why Azad described Muslims as the 'second' majority in later years. In his famous book *India Wins Freedom*, Azad argued that Partition has reduced the political capacity of Muslims. He writes:

> The only result of the creation of Pakistan was to weaken the position of the Muslims in the subcontinent of India. The 45 million Muslims who have remained in India have been weakened. On the other hand, there is as yet no indication that a strong and efficient government can be established in Pakistan. If one judges the question only from the point of view of the Muslim community, can anybody deny today that Pakistan has been for them a very unfortunate and unhappy development?[29]

The three paradoxes of Muslimness

The story of Muslims as numbers, I argue, does not stop here. It takes new shapes and forms in postcolonial India. The following chapters will unfold the various layers of this story. However, the brief discussion we have had so far may introduce us to three important paradoxes which are deeply associated with the Muslims of postcolonial India.

One or many? Many, and yet one?

Documentations on Muslims show that there are a number of Islamic communities in India who describe themselves as Muslims in a variety of ways. The existence of caste and the practice of untouchability among Muslims is observed and recognized by many colonial and Indian scholars. The census reports, anthropological studies on Muslims and even those who have surveyed the old and ancient monuments of the country tell us that it would be impossible to find any cultural similarity that unites Muslims as a community in the modern sense of the term. However, this crucial finding is ignored and, officially, Muslims are defined as a distinct legal, religious and cultural category. Interestingly, the dominant Muslim political elite continue to use this closed and integrated picture of Islam/Muslims.

Constructed Islam versus lived spirituality

The religious reform movements among Muslims, especially the evolution of sharia as a legal entity, draw their inspirations from colonial modernity. These movements, including the Deoband movement which eventually paved the way for the known pro-Congress organizations such as Jamiat Ulama-e-Hind and leaders such as Maulana Azad and Husain Ahmad Madani, produced a fully worked out imagination of Islam which was comparable with British modern English education. This Islam had a well-defined history, which could be compared with the modern history of various nations and religions; it had a distinct system of law, the sharia, which was to be juxtaposed with modern civil law; it had a sacred book, the Quran, which could be presented as a divine constitution; and it had a figure of the Prophet, whose acts and deeds are fixed in history. This systemic image of Islam was very different from the local beliefs, rituals and the everyday world of spirituality, which is followed and practised at the lower levels of society. The constructed Islam of reform movements survives as a public entity, while the lived Islam(s) of everyday type is/are completely marginalized.

Muslim issues as Muslim politics

The unified and homogeneous picture of the Muslims of India also produced a set of issues known as 'Muslim issues'. In colonial India, this set of issues was called the Muslim problem—an obstacle that was presented by the British as one of the most important justifications of the Raj. They argued that Muslims were a problem because if there weren't any Muslims/ Islam in India, it would have been much easier to work out a Hindu nation state of the European kind. The Muslim question in the British political imagination was not a solvable issue. The *Muslim question* was transformed into *Muslim issues* in the post-Partition period, though Muslim issues are also envisaged as *problems*. Eventually, the protection of Urdu, the minority character of Aligarh Muslim University, personal law, triple talaq, Babri Masjid and the burkha/purdah emerge as purely Muslim issues. This dominant imagination of Muslim political identity fits very well with different political ideologies. For instance, the Congress and other so-called secular parties use the portrayal of *pukka* Musalman to nurture their 'protection of minority' agenda, while the BJP (and the erstwhile Bharatiya Jana Sangh!) employ this Muslimness strategically to consolidate and strengthen their core Hindutva constituency. Competitive electoral politics reproduces these fixed images of 'Muslims as a political community' and we are left with a strange and somehow stupid question: *Can a Muslim be an Indian?*

These three paradoxes, I suggest, continue to survive—not merely in the political speeches of Muslim leaders like Jinnah and Azad in the 1940s but also in the recent discussions on Muslim identity. Ramachandra Guha's forceful assertion that Indian Muslims had only three progressive leaders in postcolonial India is a good example. Like Azad and Jinnah, Guha sees Muslims *merely as numbers, whose Islam is well-understood and who should be held responsible for not producing progressive leaders.*

It worth noting that Guha's selective use of Ambedkar to justify his sweeping generalizations is equally puzzling. Ambedkar did not blame Muslim men for purdah! Nor did he feel that Islam was the main problem behind women's subjugation. Ambedkar evokes Muslim plurality as a framework and situates it in the specific political context of the 1940s. He argues:

It seems to me that the reason for the absence of the spirit of change in the Indian Musalman is to be sought in the peculiar position he occupies in India. He is placed in a social environment which is predominantly Hindu. That Hindu environment is always silently but surely encroaching upon him. He feels that it is de-musalmanizing him. As a protection against this gradual weaning away, he is led to insist on preserving everything that is Islamic without caring to examine whether it is helpful or harmful to his society.[30]

Ambedkar further states:

Muslims in India are placed in a political environment which is also predominantly Hindu. He feels that he will be suppressed and that political suppression will make the Muslims a depressed class. It is this consciousness that he has to save himself from being submerged by the Hindus socially and politically, which to my mind is the primary cause why the Indian Muslims [. . .] are backward in the matter of social reform.[31]

In my view, Ambedkar was probably the first and only political commentator of the 1940s who talks of Muslim caste, the Muslim practice of untouchability and the subjugation of Muslim women in relation to the dominant Muslim elites' quest for protected representation and the Hindu elites' anti-Muslim communal politics. His argument not only reminds us of the crucial difference between the Muslim elite and Muslim masses, it also explains the fact that Hindu communalism is one of the most important reasons behind Muslim backwardness.

Ambedkar, in this sense, pushes us to go beyond the dominant story of 'Muslims as numbers' and the paradoxes associated with Muslim identity. However, it is important to remember that the questions of Ambedkar were very different from our questions. He is certainly very relevant to us, but at the same time, the mere worshipping of Ambedkar would not solve our purpose. We must extract a framework out of his observations. This is what I wish to do in this book.

I address Muslims not as numbers but as a constitutional category, a religious minority and as a collectivity in two different senses. In a positive sense, I use Muslims as a collectivity when individuals with Muslim names and/or groups, who prefer to call themselves Islamic, are recognized as a beneficiary of constitutionally granted collective rights, such as the right to profess religion and the right to protect culture and heritage. However, I also use Muslims as a collectivity in a negative sense, particularly when individuals with Muslim names and legally recognized minority institutions with Islamic contents are threatened and attacked especially by Hindutva essentialists. In both cases, the term 'Muslim' is used as a generic, unspecified expression, which acquires various concrete meanings only when it is employed in everyday conversations. Hence, there is a need to examine 'Muslim' as a term in relation to Muslim caste systems and untouchability, economic disparity and the class structure of Muslim societies in India, the Muslim forms of patriarchy and gender relations and, finally, the regional/linguistic conflicts among Muslims. This workable conceptualization of Muslimness, I hope, can help us in examining the political manifestation of the three paradoxes of postcolonial Muslim identity, which we have outlined in this chapter.

2

Muslims as a Religious Community

'Pukka Musalman'

On 20 August 2018, an interesting video clip was posted on Twitter by a user with the handle @AnuMishraBJP. (This Twitter account carries a picture of Rohit Sardana, a Zee TV journalist. Later, it was claimed to be a fake Twitter account.)

In this fifteen-second video, a teenage boy tears the Indian national flag and says: 'Pakka Musalman hoon.'[1]

The tweet, which is in Hindi, elaborates on the video and asks a question:

भारत के राष्ट्रीय ध्वज को फाड़ के फेंक दिया इस लड़के ने कह रहा है . . . कि 'पक्का मुसलमान हूँ' ये मानसिकता कहाँ से पैदा हो रही है ? @sardanarohit @ KapilMishra_IND @TajinderBagga
(Tearing and throwing away the national flag of India, this boy is saying that . . . 'I am a true Muslim.' What is the source of this mentality?)

As expected, the video was widely circulated on social media. Pro-Hindutva Twitter handles used the video to demonstrate the fact that Indian Muslims do not respect the Indian flag—the most revered symbol of our patriotism.

The story does not end here. Another video was uploaded on Twitter and other social media on the same day. In this second video, the boy is beaten up by a group of people, who eventually force him to apologize and say 'Bharat Mata ki Jai' and 'Main Pukka Hindu Hoon'.

This video was reposted by the editor-in-chief of Sudarshan News, Suresh Chavhanke. He also wrote an explanatory tweet in Hindi:

पक्का मुसलमान हूँ इसलिए तिरंगा फाड़ के फेंकने वाला 'स्वामी अग्निवेश' संस्कार होते ही#भारत_माता_की_जयबोल कर नारे देने लगा। लातों के भूत बातों से नहीं मानते। अब कोई कहेगा कि ये तो #Lynching है पर कोई यह भी बताए कि संविधान इस को कैसे रोक सकता है? कानून तो इनको रोकने में विफल है!

(The moment this boy was given the 'Swami Agniwesh–type treatment', he started shouting 'Bharat Mata ki Jai'. Some people really deserve this treatment. One may say that this is #lynching; but please enlighten us how does the Constitution bring an end to such events. After all, the law has completely failed.)[2]

It is obvious that 'Swami Agnivesh–type treatment' was referring to the lynching of those individuals who do not subscribe to the ideas of radical Hindutva. The boy, who is shown as a Muslim in this video, was lynched in a similar manner to make him truly patriotic/Indian/a pukka Hindu.

Interestingly, this boy later turned out to be a Hindu! This incident took place in Surat, Gujarat. Surat police traced the boy and his friend, who actually filmed him, and circulated the video (though it was not clear whether the video was actually uploaded on Twitter by this boy or not).

In a statement given to Alt News, the police inspector, Amroli police station, Surat, clarified, 'Both the teenagers are friends and belong to the Hindu community. The boys have also apologized for acting childishly.'[3]

The episode did not die down. The two videos are available on Twitter and no one has apologized for this fake propaganda.

Although the proliferation of such news and videos on social media has now become the new normal, the way in which the binary between good Muslims and the patriotic Indian has been established in this incident is quite instructive. The lawlessness in the name of 'pukka Hindu' is justified and presented as the most acceptable reaction to the pukka Musalman phenomenon.

'Pukka Musalman' refers to two related aspects of Muslim identity: religious commitment and patriotism. The religious commitment of Muslims is often underlined by emphasizing the fact that Muslims are more religious than other communities. It is strongly asserted that this commitment is so powerful and overarching that it does not allow them to pay respect to any other social affiliation. As a result, the mentality of disrespecting the national flag can be said to come from Islamic teachings!

The second aspect of the pukka Musalman concept is related to the post–British Raj story of South Asia. The partition of British India on a religious basis is understood through the prism of the European-style nation state. It is believed that the European model of state based on 'one religion, one culture and one ethnicity' is the ideal mode to realize the real and enduring form of nationalism. Following this dominant perception, a very simplistic conclusion is drawn: Muslims as a community, which follows Islam as a religion, were able to achieve Pakistan—a Muslim nation state. But the Hindus could not get a Hindu Rashtra in India despite being a majority. The success story of Muslims (and the evident failure of Hindus) is also attributed to the idea of pukka Musalman—the strong sense of community and religiosity among Muslims. The VHP's famous slogan 'Garv se Kaho Hum Hindu Hai' (Say proudly I am a Hindu!) must be seen as an attempt to create a community of pukka Hindus!

The imagination of a pukka Musalman as a religious, committed person survives in various spheres of postcolonial Indian public life. Be it the devoted, god-fearing Musalman of the Hindi cinema of the 1970s and/or the contemporary radical jihadists, Muslims are always portrayed as a community of religious, committed individuals. This portrayal of Islamist Muslims requires a critical assessment. We must ask two crucial sets of questions: First, what are the self-perceptions of Muslims about Islam? Do they consider themselves religiously committed? Are Muslim self-perceptions different from those of other religious communities? Second, do all Muslims in India practise Islam in the same way? Does social stratification among Muslims affect their religiosity?

Pukka Musalman and the five pillars

This stated commitment of India's Muslims for Islam cannot be understood without discussing the basic component of Islamic religiosity: the rituals and practices. For this purpose, we can begin with the famous 'Five Pillar theory', which is often presented to Muslims as well as non-Muslims as the most reliable, authentic formulation of Islam. This assessment of religiosity will help us in making sense of the two most frequently used terms: namaz and *roza*.

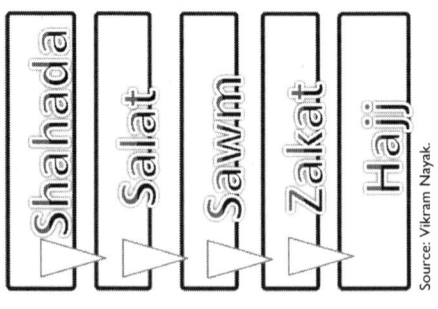

The five pillars of Islam.

Let us look at the figure on the previous page. It introduces us to the five basic principles which constitute Islam. Both Shia and Sunni Islam adhere to these five pillars, though they continue to follow their own interpretations. The first pillar is called Shahada in Arabic (Shahadat in Urdu/Hindustani). It means sincerely reciting the Kalima to express commitment to the Oneness of God (Allah) and the prophethood of Muhammad. The Kalima is:

Laaa Ilaaha Illa-llaahu Muhammadur-Rasoolu-llaah
(There is none worthy of worship except Allah, and Muhammad is the Messenger of Allah)

The Salat (namaz in Urdu/Persian) is the second pillar. It is about performing prayers five times in a day. These prayers are: Fajr (prayer before sunrise), Zuhr (afternoon prayer), Asr (late-afternoon prayer), Maghrib (prayer immediately after sunset) and Isha (late-evening prayer). These prayers can be offered individually; however, it is advised that Muslims offer them collectively as a congregation. The weekly Friday-afternoon prayer and the annual Eid prayers (Eid ur Fitr and Eid ul-Azha) are congressional prayers. This is followed by the third pillar, Sawm (roza in Urdu/Persian). Muslims are instructed by the Quran to observe fast in the Islamic month of Ramzan. The next two pillars are not obligatory for all Muslims. The Zakat is a type of charity that is compulsory only for rich and wealthy Muslims. Similarly, the Hajj—the annual pilgrimage to the city of Mecca—is also subject to financial capabilities of a person.

If we look closely at the sequence of these pillars of Islam, we may find three different forms of commitments: verbal, bodily and financial. Since the financial commitment is not applicable to all Muslims, verbal expressions of faith and bodily acts of worship form the structure of the innermost domain of Islamic belief systems. For instance, the belief that there is only one God, Allah, and Muhammad is the Prophet of Allah is a verbally expressed commitment. Muslims are asked to not merely recite this Kalima frequently, but to also try to imbibe it in their everyday life. The Urdu word *shahadat*, which means 'to witness', actually captures the spirit of this form of Islamic commitment.

The namaz and roza are the actual ritualistic practices which are performed through bodily actions. This inherent performative aspect transforms these two pillars of Islam into a symbol of bodily commitment. Let us first take namaz as an example to illustrate this point.

Despite the fact that the five pillars of Islam do not follow any particular hierarchy, the namaz has emerged as one of the most fundamental Islamic religious rituals. Every Muslim adult (except a few, such as children, women during their menstruation period, the terminally ill, etc.) is required to offer namaz five times a day. To perform namaz, one has to clean the visible parts of the body with water, which is called *wadu* (ablutions). This is followed by the actual act of namaz. The worshipper is expected to pray, either alone or in congregation, in the direction of Kaaba. This act establishes a direct relationship between the devotee's body and the sacred sites of Islam.

The duration of namaz and the style of performing it are also related to each other. The term *rakah* is used to mention the duration of prayer as well as the actions prescribed in order to perform the namaz. For example, the morning namaz is called Fajr that has a total of four rakah, while the late-evening prayer called Isha has seventeen rakah. In each rakah, the worshipper follows a given cycle of actions (standing, prostrating, kneeling, sitting), which are performed with fixed narrations of Quranic and non-Quranic Islamic recitations, called *dua*s in Arabic. The following figure shows the act of namaz.

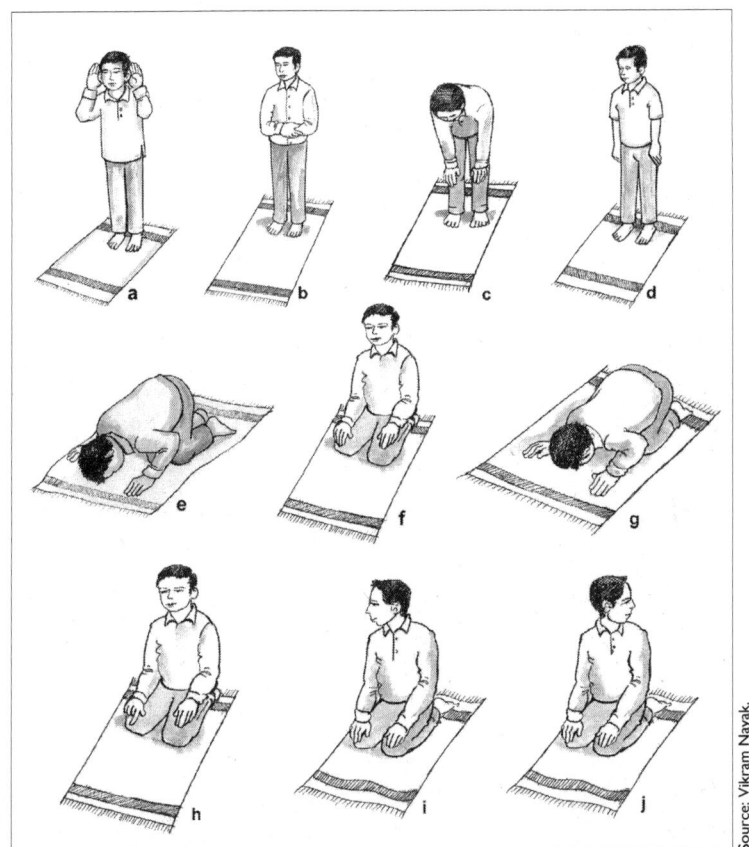

Source: Vikram Nayak.

Namaz as a performative commitment (Hanafi Maslak).

Since namaz is an obligatory ritual, it serves two functions—it is a responsibility to face Allah five times a day in person and, at the same time, it is the mode by which a worshipper is expected to establish a balance between bodily actions and his/her thought processes. In other words, a worshipper has not only to execute namaz in a given format of actions with a set recitation of texts, but at the same time, he/she is expected to put himself/herself in an imaginary state of mind where Allah is supposedly looking at him/her.

These performative aspects of namaz are quite theatrical. This is a theatre-like situation where an actor has not only to perform through dialogues and bodily actions but also put his/her mind in the character which he/she is trying to enact. Thus, spirituality, Islamic thought seems to suggest, can be achieved if and only if an equilibrium is established between the performance of bodily acts and the imaginations prescribed behind these acts.

This is also applicable to the act of roza. It is obligatory (*farz*) for adult Muslims to observe a fast during the month of Ramzan (except those who are suffering from an illness, those who are travelling, those cannot fast due to old age and women who are pregnant, breastfeeding or menstruating). Observing roza from dawn to sunset is not just about refraining from food, drink, smoking and sexual intercourse. It is expected from the *rozedar* (the person who observes the fast) that he/she must not get involved in any sinful behaviour and must observe his/her roza as an instrument to purify his/her spiritual engagement with Allah. In this sense, the physical act of fasting is a means to achieve moral–spiritual ends.

Three broad inferences can be drawn from the discussion:

• There is an agreement that the five pillars constitute Islam as a religion and all sects of Islam recognize them as fundamental features. However, they continue to offer varied interpretations of these pillars to legitimize their own modes of rituals and practices. This may be the reason why Salat becomes namaz and Sawm becomes roza for Urdu/Persian-speaking Muslim communities. In other words, the Five Pillar theory does not disregard the religious plurality within Islam.

• There are three kinds of commitments a Muslims is expected to make: verbal, bodily and financial. Since bodily commitments are the most visible form of religious practices, the namaz and roza have emerged as the most fundamental aspects of Islamic religiosity.

- The bodily commitment, expressed through the practices of namaz and roza, cannot be completed without absolute devotion to the ideas and principles associated with these acts.

The Five Pillar theory, we must remember, offers us an ideal picture of Islam. It does not tell us the multiple modes in which these aspects of religion are formed, reformed and even negated in the everyday life of Muslims in various contexts. To understand this dilemma between the theory of Islam and the practices of Muslims, we need to go beyond this textual description of Islam and look at the perceptions and views of Muslims about it. The question is: Do Muslims consider themselves pukka Musalman in contemporary India?

Pukka Musalman versus 'somewhat religious' Muslims

Sample survey as a method, in my view, is the most appropriate technique to evaluate the level of religiosity among Muslims in India for two very practical reasons. First, the survey method is useful in reaching out to a large number of Muslims who live in different geographical locations. Second, the survey method can also help in evaluating the consistency and divergence of opinions, views and perceptions. However, it all depends on the rigour of methodology, especially the sampling exercise.

Keeping these considerations in mind, the Centre for the Study of Developing Societies (CSDS)-Lokniti's Religious Attitude and Practices Survey 2015—an all-India study covering twenty-one states, with a sample size of 5681 respondents—explored the 'pukka Musalman' phenomenon.

The findings of the survey were quite instructive. Muslims do not think that they are 'very religious'. Instead, most of them feel that they may well be described as 'somewhat religious' (see Table 1 on p. 40). This Muslim self-perception cannot simply be called a reflection of minority psyche.

In fact, two other religious minorities—Sikhs and Christians—appear more confident than Muslims in asserting their religiosity. The Indian Christian community actually emerges as the most religious social group of the country.

On the contrary, one finds a striking similarity between Hindu and Muslim opinion. Despite significant differences between the modes of worship and the nature of religiosity between Hinduism and Islamic traditions, the majority of Hindu and Muslim respondents do not consider themselves sufficiently religious.

This somewhat religious attitude of Muslims must be seen in a wider perspective. Contemporary Islamic religious debates, especially among Sunnis, are more concerned about the growing worldly outlook of Muslims. The decline of Islamic pre-eminence in the contemporary world is seen as a direct outcome of non-Islamic values and practices. Although the meanings of the true Islamic path and the modes to achieve it have been an unsettled issue, there is a consensus that to 'go back to the original Islam' would be the ultimate solution. Take, for example, the Tablighi Jamaat, which has emerged as one of the most powerful forms of ritualistic Islam in the last three decades. The adherents of the Jamaat are encouraged to give up politics to devote themselves completely to preparing Muslims for the next world. This is why the Jamaat invites Muslims for '*deen ki mehnat*' (struggle to consolidate faith).

This overtly apolitical form of contemporary Islam functions in two different ways. Muslims are told that their spiritual beliefs as well as religious practices are not adequately Islamic; therefore, they must give up unnecessary worldly considerations and consolidate their Islamic commitment. At the same time, they are also asked to create a balance between *deen* and *duniya* (religion and this world), following the example of the early Islamic society of Prophet Muhammad. In this sense, Islam is introduced as a possibility, which would persuade somewhat religious Muslims into becoming very religious ones in the course of time.

The practice of religion by Muslims further substantiates this point. Namaz and roza are not observed uniformly by all Muslims. These practices as rituals, no doubt, are highly diversified (especially the namaz) and every sect has its own tradition, but it is also true that Muslims do not follow them on a regular basis. There is even a crucial distinction between OBC (Other Backward Class) Muslims and Muslims from the general category. OBC Muslims appear to practise the religion more than Muslim upper-caste members do, which again goes against established public wisdom that universalizes Islam and Muslims uncritically!

Obviously, it is not possible to make any grand observation about the societal attitudes of Muslim communities on the basis of these findings. But it could certainly be argued that Islamic religiosities do not entirely determine the everyday life of Indian Muslim communities. That is the reason why they describe themselves as 'somewhat religious'. The changing nature of Islamic religiosities also plays a role. Islam refashions itself in order to adjust with the requirements of the secular state. The evocation of 'deen ki mehnat' by Tablighi Jamaat, instead of direct politics, is a good example of this Islamic recasting. We shall discuss this aspect in greater detail in the next chapter.

Nevertheless, the tussle between common Muslims and the religious elite has always been an important aspect of Islamic religious discourse in India. This is what poet Altaf Hussain Hali identified back in the 1890s. He wrote:

Barbe jis se nafrat vob taqreer karni
Jigar jis se sha bon vob tebrir karni
Gunahagaar bandon ki tebqreer karni
Musalman bhai ki takfeer karni
Ye bai aalimon ka bamaare tareeqa
Ye hai baadiyon ka hammare saleeqa
(Make speeches that will only hatred enhance

Write tracts which violate all decent norms
Insult and degrade, never pardon perchance
Call Muslims 'you *kafirs*', swagger and strut
This is the method of our religious crusaders
Our leaders in this are the shrewdest of traders.)

Koi mas'ala poochhne un se jaaye
To gardan pe baar-e-garaan le kea aye
Agar badnaseebi se shak us mein laaye
To qate'ee khitab abl-e-dozakh ka paaye
Agar aiteraaz uska nikla zabaan se
To aana salaamat hai dushwaar wan se.
(If a question arises which one asks them about
Then with a dead weight on his neck he returns
And if the unfortunate posts a doubt
Then doubtless to Hell he is straightaway sent
If a word of dissent ever escapes his lips
Then to safely return is not part of this trip.)[4]

Table 1: How religious are Indians?

	Very religious	Somewhat religious	Not religious at all	No response
Hindus	30	59	5	6
Muslims	29	57	4	10
Christian	45	50	2	3
Sikhs	35	58	-	7

Source: Religious Attitudes and Practices Survey 2015, by CSDS-Lokniti
Data Unit
Figures are in percentages

Table 2: The Islam(s) of Muslims

	Regularly	Occasionally	Once in a few days/ Observe irregularly	Never	No response
Offer Namaz					
Muslim OBC	52	31	7	9	1
Muslim General	38	40	11	10	1
Keep Fast (Roza)					
Muslim OBC	45	41	10	3	1
Muslim General	45	38	10	5	2

Source: Religious Attitudes and Practices Survey 2015, CSDS-Lokniti Data Unit
Figures are in percentages

3

'Islamization' since Independence!

'Dawat-e-Islam' and/or 'conversion'?

In 1981, an unusual event took place in a small village in Tamil Nadu, which actually redefined the public image of Indian Islam in an unprecedented manner. Around 180 Pallan Dalit families of Meenakshipuram—a hamlet of the Thenpoti panchayat in the Tenkasi taluk of Tirunelveli district of Tamil Nadu—decided to embrace Islam. This conversion, as various detailed ethnographic studies of this event show, was a highly localized affair. It was found that the upward mobility of the Scheduled Caste (SC) communities of Meenakshipuram and the ongoing resistance to the practice of untouchability at the local level were the two main reasons behind this mass conversion.[1] However, the local experience of the event somehow evaporated gradually and the Meenakshipuram episode transformed into a civilizational conflict between Islam and Hinduism.

As expected, the most interesting reaction came from the RSS. An official resolution passed by the RSS in 1982 asserts that:

> Many underhand tactics being adopted by the Muslim proselytizers such as aggravation and exploitation of 'untouchability', the lure of so-called equality in Islam [. . .] as against the discrimination in

42

the Hindu fold, instigation of police against the Harijans, promises of security in the Muslim fold because of political favouritism, and dangling of lucrative jobs in oil-rich Muslim countries [. . .] Experience of past history amply bears out the fact that such conversions do not merely imply a simple change in way of worship, but destruction of national culture and sentiments, growth of separatist and secessionist tendencies and extra-territorial loyalties and communal animosities and flare-ups as well, which directly strike at the roots of our national integrity and security. As such, the problem of such conversions should be a matter of serious concern for all our patriotic and nationalist people.[2]

The resolution makes two interesting points. Questioning the practice of Islamic conversion, it is argued that untouchability is exploited by the Muslim preachers to mislead Dalits. It is also alleged that the converted Dalits were promised jobs in rich Muslim countries; hence, the act of conversion could not entirely be called 'spiritual'.

The outcome of conversion is the second problematic area. The resolution says that conversion to Islam in India will destroy the 'national culture' of the country. By this definition of national culture, the Indian version of Islam cannot be called an authentic Indian faith system. Therefore, we are told that the conversion to Islam will inevitably lead to separatism, communalism and extraterritorial loyalties. It implies that if someone becomes Muslim (even though forcibly!), he/she would imbibe the ideology of anti-Indian separatism and his/her future conduct would always be determined by his/her faith in Islam. To counter these anti-national tendencies, the resolution asks the government to implement a strict anti-conversion law.

It is true that these kind of polemical documents are mainly published and disseminated by Hindu nationalists to carve a space for themselves in the public sphere. But the popular discussion on the aggressive conversion of non-Muslims into the Islamic fold cannot entirely be called the invention of Hindutva politics. The colonial history of India, which presented India's past as a battleground of religious wars, actually popularized this story of Islamization. The belief that Muslims came from 'outside' and forcibly converted Hindus in the medieval period concretized as a fact and contributed a lot in the making of modern Muslim identities in the subcontinent. The central component of Islamic faith—*dawat* (or what is also known as 'Dawat-e-Islam' in popular Hindustani, which means inviting individuals and communities to embrace Islam)—thus emerges as a contentious issue.

This contention is not accidental. There are verses in the Quran which encourage believers to spread the message of Allah. (See Box 1 below.) After all, the Quran is revealed for the entire humanity—not solely for the community of believers called 'Muslims'. The distinction between *being Muslim* and *becoming Muslim* is not very relevant. Does it mean that Dawat-e-Islam is nothing but a strategy to convert non-Muslims, so as to increase Muslim population? Does it mean that the kind of Islam Muslims practise in India cannot be completed without the act of conversion? Does it mean that there is a design behind events such as the Meenakshipuram episode?

Box 1: Dawat in the Quran

'Invite (people) to the way of your lord with wisdom and good counsel.' (Verse: 16:125)

'And there has to be a group of people from among you who call towards good and prevent from evil.' (Verse: 3:104)

'And who is better in utterance than the one who called people towards Allah, and acts righteously and says, "I am one of those who submit themselves (to Allah)."' (Verse: 41:33)

Source: The Holy Quran

These questions force us to revisit the postcolonial story of Indian Islam from the vantage point of Islamic dawat. This is what this chapter is all about. It examines the ideas of three prominent Sunni religious figures, Maulana Abul Ala Hasan Ali Nadwi (also known as Ali Mian), Maulana Wahiduddin Khan and Zakir Naik, and the activities of two leading Sunni movements, Tablighi Jamaat and Jamaat-e-Islami Hind (JIH).

The choice of these figures and movements for a discussion of this kind is not entirely arbitrary. Maulana Ali Mian (d. 1999), Maulana Wahiduddin Khan and Zakir Naik have a profound impact on contemporary Indian public life. Ali Mian helped the government to draft the infamous Muslim Women (Protection of Rights on Divorce) Act, 1986, in the wake of the Shah Bano controversy. He was again appointed by the government to represent the 'Muslim position' on the Babri Masjid in 1989. In contrast, Maulana Wahiduddin Khan is often recognized as a 'progressive and liberal' Muslim religious leader. Interestingly, his version of Islam also revolves around the idea of dawat. Zakir Naik is a relatively recent phenomenon. His mode of Dawat-e-Islam deviates significantly from those of other religious groups and leaders in postcolonial India. His *on-line/image-centric technocratic Islam* makes him a very powerful figure.

This is also true about JIH—a recognized and registered Muslim organization which works primarily as a pressure group. JIH was banned by the government in 1948 and later again in 1993. Although the Constitution of the JIH defines it as a 'secular' religious organization committed to work within the ambit of constitutionally defined minority rights, the political ideas of its founder and ideologue Maulana Abul Ala Maududi (who migrated to Pakistan in 1947) makes it an interesting case study of Dawat-e-Islam. On the other hand, Tablighi Jamaat is an Islamic religious reform movement. It has emerged as one of the most dominant forms of religiosity in postcolonial India. This loosely organized organization offers us a very different form of Islam. The adherents of the Jamaat are encouraged to avoid all references to politics and asked to devote themselves to 'deen ki mehnat'.

Islam as dawat in modern India

We have to trace our story of Indian Islam from the nineteenth century. The post-1857 debates on Islamic dawat were the outcomes of a long process of religious reconstitution of Islamic religiosity— the codification of Islamic principles on an entirely modern basis and an elusive search for an ideal practice, which could rejuvenate Islam as a way of life. This process of religious revival led to two crucial questions:

(a) How to re-establish Islamic supremacy, making it the ultimate religion in a colonial context?
(b) How to invite Muslims to give up un-Islamic practices and embrace ideal Islam?

The decline of Islamic pre-eminence in modern times, interestingly, was not seen as an end result of the fall of Muslim rule in India in these religious debates. Instead, the weakening of Muslim political power was conceived as an inevitable consequence of the non-Islamic values and cultural practices of Muslims. The argument that the status and prestige of Muslims in India (as elsewhere) is weakened because Muslims had given up the true path of Islam seems to dominate the religious discussions of the late nineteenth and early twentieth century. Although the meaning of the true Islamic path and the modes to achieve it had always been a highly contested issue, there was a consensus that the revival of the original, ideal Islam would be the ultimate solution.

The pro-empire Muslim elite, such as Syed Ahmad Khan (the founder of Aligarh Muslim University), evoked the inherent liberal and scientific spirit of original Islamic principles to carve out a political space for Muslims in the colonial institutional framework.[3] This religious reinterpretation legitimized the reform agenda of modern education in later years. On the other hand, the anti-empire Muslim elite, especially the ulema associated with Deoband, highlighted the revolutionary potential of original Islam. This radical elucidation of Islam produced a powerful conceptualization of '*mutahidda qaumiyat*' (unified/composite nationalism)—an assertion that true Islam permits Muslims to make collations with other religious groups for the sake of territorial nationalism.[4] These seemingly different Islamic explanations focused primarily on the reconversion of Muslims—the assertion that in order to establish Islamic supremacy, there is a need to make Muslims more Islamic.

Three main ideas were advanced with regard to the objective of Dawat-e-Islam in the late colonial period. There was a dominant view that Islam should be presented as a modern religion that is capable of answering the challenges posed by modernity. Thus, the purpose of dawat, according to this thesis, was twofold—Muslims should be educated so that they could appreciate the universal spirit of Islam, and non-Muslims must be introduced to Islam for opening up the scope for rational intellectual debates.

This adherence to education found a very different expression in the thesis proposed by the conventional ulema. This second influential thesis of dawat relied heavily on the purity of ideas and practices and argued for spreading religious education through the network of mosques, *maktab*s and madrasas. This institutionalization was seen as a means of spreading Islam among Muslims.[5] The third thesis suggested a clear separation of religion from overtly political affairs so as to work on the commitment-building of Muslims. This thesis was advocated mainly by Maulana Mohammad Ilyas, the founder of Tablighi Jamaat.[6]

These three versions of Dawat-e-Islam found new meanings in post-Partition India, especially after the creation of Pakistan. The speech delivered by Maulana Maududi, the founder of Jamaat-e-Islami, in Madras (now Chennai) on 26 April 1947, a few months before the partition of South Asia, must be seen in this perspective. Maududi explores possibilities of the propagation of Islam in the future republic of India in this speech by offering a blueprint of what he calls 'a peaceful Islamic revolution'.

Maududi made four proposals. The first two suggestions were concerned with creating a conducive environment for spreading the message of Islam—a trust-building endeavour so as to carve out a space for Dawat-e-Islam in India. He says:

> Confidence is to be reposed in the Hindu nationalist movement through our course of action that there is no other religion competing with them politically [. . .] the [. . .] important task for us is to spread Islamic knowledge on a wide scale among Muslims, create in them a general desire for propagation of Islam and reform of their character and social lives to an extent where non-Muslims will feel their society to be clearly better than their own.[7]

The other two proposals were concerned with the appropriate strategy for effective Dawat-e-Islam in future India. Maududi argues that preparing Islamic intellectuals and the translation of Islamic literature in Indian languages could be two crucial aspects of dawat. He advises: 'Our workers [. . .] should learn [. . .] Indian languages [. . .] If Muslims restrict themselves only to Urdu due to their religious prejudice, they will become strangers to the general population to the nation.'[8]

This blueprint of Islamic revolution, I suggest, introduces us to three central aspects of postcolonial Islamic religiosity: the meanings and purpose of religion, the identified constituency for religious mobilization and the possible modes by which the message of Islam could effectively be disseminated.

Islamic scholars, religious movements and Muslim political elites offer a variety of different (and most times conflicting) answers to fundamental issues. Interestingly, these varied responses do not always remain fixed: arguments change, positions modify and sometimes a completely new resolve is proposed. To map out this discursively constituted discourse, let us identify five different responses and read them in relation to the postcolonial Indian debate on freedom of religion.

Dawat for the sake of dawat

Maulana Mohammad Yusuf, the second amir (head) of Tablighi Jamaat and the successor of Mohammad Ilyas, describes Dawat-e-Islam as an end in itself.[9] Defining the meanings of dawat, he says: 'The manner in which Prophet Muhammad lived his life and worked for the deen of Allah is tabligh.'[10]

It does not, however, mean that this simple and uncomplicated notion of Dawat-e-Islam is entirely purposeless. Yusuf reminds us:

> Roman and Persian empires were like the webs of a spider at the time of Prophet Muhammad. The Prophet worked on the commitment-building of Muslims and prepared pure believers. Because of the shared presence of these pure believers, Allah cleaned the webs of Rome and Persia with his *azab* (punishment). This is eventually going to happen with the superpowers of our time: Russia and USA.[11]

Deen (religion), in this framework of dawat, is juxtaposed with duniya (world). It is argued that deen is an expression of faith and commitment in Allah, which can only be completed by absorbing the message of the Prophet. Muslims need to consolidate deen if they want to achieve success in this life and in life after death.[12]

Thus, Muslims should not endeavour to establish Islamic dominance (in direct political terms) in this world. Instead, they should act (*amal*) to consolidate deen through Dawat-e-Islam—inviting others to Islam. Yusuf claims:

> The purpose of tabligh is not to disseminate any particular form of knowledge; instead, the aim is to breathe life into the very idea of deen that the Prophet brought in and make it actable for the prosperity of Muslims. If this very idea triumphs as a part and parcel of everyday life, the Almighty would shower his kindness on us.[13]

To understand the nature of this 'dawat for deen', one needs to unfold the Tablighi Jamaat's famous six principles:

- *Kalima* (profession of faith)
- *Salat* (five times prayers or *namaz*)
- *Ilm-o-Ziikr* (knowledge and remembrance of God)
- *Ikram-i Muslim* (respect of every Muslim)
- *Ikhlas-i niyyat* (sincerity of intention)
- *Tafrigh-i waqt* (sparing time)

The first three principles focus on the universally accepted norms of Islamic religiosity. One must have faith in the Kalima, one must offer Salat five times a day and one must recite the Quran (or for that matter any other religious text). However, the last three principles are quite innovative, which underlines the argument Yusuf makes. For instance, the principle of Ikram-i Muslim calls upon Muslims (and particularly those who are involved in Jamaat's work) to show respect to all forms of Islamic religious practices and avoid those actions which may lead to religious arguments and confrontations. The principle of Ikhlas-i niyyat is about the individual's intention to participate in the activities of Jamaat. If the intention is sincere, it is argued, Allah would help the person to translate intentions into action. The last principle, Tafrigh-i waqt (sparing time), is an extension of the purity-of-intention principle, which tells us how to put words and intentions into action.[14]

What is really striking in this schema is the focus on amal (action). Jamaat makes a persuasive argument to abandon the given meaning of Islam as an individual-centric spiritual experience. Instead, it offers a systematic plan of action to get involved collectively in world affairs for preparing Muslims for the hereafter. This unequivocal appeal for religious transformation is an appropriate example of 'propagation of religion' in the strictly Indian legal–constitutional sense. In fact, this form of Dawat-e-Islam moves away from all possible kinds of social and/or political interventions and serves to protect the *iman* (belief) of those who have already recognized themselves as Muslims![15]

Dawat-e-Islam as an assertion of identity

Jamaat-e-Islami does not approve of this overtly apolitical dawat of Tablighi Jamaat.[16] Without describing itself as a political organization, the JIH evokes Dawat-e-Islam as a mode to intervene in the postcolonial public sphere. Two examples are relevant in elaborating on this form of religious–political intervention. Maulana Abul Lais Islahi Nadwi (the amir of the JIH in the 1950s) delivered a speech in 1952 in Hyderabad, outlining the features of the JIH's da'wa project. He argues:

> JIH is not a religious organization in the restricted sense of the term; nor is it a political group in the way politics is popularly understood [. . .] we invite people to worship Almighty. We have not only given da'wa to Muslims but have made serious endeavour to introduce it (Islamic teachings) to each and every community of India. For this purpose we have started producing

literature in languages other than Urdu [. . .] We do not want to assemble a huge crowd; instead, we attempt to want conformity of ideas. When they (people) recognize the truthfulness of our message, they would redesign their lives accordingly.[17]

Like Tablighi Jamaat, the JIH also recognizes the centrality of dawat as an important aspect of Islamic religiosity. But at the same time, it does show an active interest in the ongoing political debates and issues concerning Muslims. In fact, the dissemination of Islam is identified as a way to get into direct political discussions. To work out a practical design for this seemingly difficult project of dawat, especially in the post-Partition, anti-Muslim environment of the 1950–1970s, JIH took the language question very seriously.

The foreword written by Maulana Maududi for the Hindi translation of the Quran in 1970 underlines this aspect. Maududi writes, 'It had been felt for a long time that there was a need for translating the Quran and other Islamic literature in Hindi, which is the national language of India [. . .] so that the vast majority of the Hindi-speaking population gets acquainted with the fundamental essence of Islam.'[18]

To understand the significance of Maududi's argument, one has to look at the manner in which the question of language and translation is debated in postcolonial India. The famous Calcutta Quran case is a good example here. In 1985, a writ petition was filed in the Calcutta High Court stating, 'The publication of the Koran in the Arabic original as well as in its translations in various languages [. . .] amounts to commission of offences [. . .] and accordingly each copy of the book must be declared as forfeited.' (Writ Petition 227 of 1985.) The petition, as expected, was dismissed by the court on the grounds that the Quran was the basic text of Islam. However, Hindu fundamentalist groups continued to use this politically motivated reading of the Quran for mobilizing Hindus.

The Hindi translation of the Quran published by the Jamiat-Ulama-e-Hind responded to this debate directly. In the preface to the Hindi version of the Quran, the translators argue that the purpose of translating the Quran into Hindi was primarily to expose the anti-Muslim propaganda of Hindu fundamentalists. They argue that 'the essentialist and anti-Muslim conclusions are quite possible only because of substandard Hindi translations of the Quran'.[19] In order to maintain the purity of Hindi, this translation of the Quran was finally sent to a few Hindi experts (who happened to be non-Muslims) for their approval!

The evolution of Hindi as a possible language of Islam in postcolonial India must be seen in the wider Hindi/Urdu politics of the 1970s.[20] The protection of Urdu, which eventually emerged as a 'minority issue' is creatively re-conceptualized by Dawat-e-Islam movements, especially by the JIH. While adherence to the protection of Urdu was profoundly expressed in this case, other Indian languages, especially Hindi, were seen as tools to spread the message of Islam. This reordering of languages helps the JIH communicate with various actors—the state, non-Muslims and non-Urdu speaking Muslim communities—within the framework of constitutionally granted freedom of religion.

Dawat-e-Islam as a 'rational choice'

Maulana Wahiduddin Khan, like Tablighi Jamaat and JIH, recognizes the centrality of dawat. He describes dawat as the natural expression of iman and makes an attempt to historicize the outcome of this sacred performance—the conversion of a large number of non-Muslims to Islam in the past. But the focus on the conversion to Islam in the contemporary world is not emphasized directly in Khan's framework. While recognizing Islam as the best, authentic and most unadulterated religion of the world, Khan offers a nuanced perspective on conversion. In his opinion:

Conversion in Islamic thought is not synonymous with proselytism in the formal sense. It is an event which takes place in a person's life as a result of intellectual revolution or spiritual transformation. It is not simply leaving one religious tradition for another. The Islamic ideal of conversion is for the individual to discover the truth after an exhaustive search for it and then by his own choice, abandon one religion for another.[21]

If the purpose of dawat is to transform a person intellectually, what are the possibilities of this kind of intellectual change of heart? Khan gives a very intriguing reply. He argues that modern rationality has become a way of life in the contemporary world. He recognizes the presence of a number of rational truth-seekers, who are exploring all sorts of possibilities to search for appropriate and rational solutions to the challenges posed by modern life. Khan says that this intellectual revolution of our times has favoured Islam because 'all other religions have been subjected to human interpolation and have been rendered historically unauthentic [. . .] Islam enjoys the exceptional position of having the authentic version of the revealed religion'.[22] In his opinion, therefore, there is a need to convert this rational search for truth into consciousness, as 'all the people of the present day have potentially become Muslims' and, therefore, 'the need of the hour is to do da'wa work [. . .] so that this potential may be turned into a reality.'[23]

The 'conducive environment', which Maududi talks of in his 1947 speech, is interpreted rather differently by Khan. He envisages an environment of rationality and identifies 'potential Muslims' in this rational world. Khan seems to suggest that conversion in a given and formal sense of the term disrupts the argument for propagation of Islam as dawat—primarily because conversion is not an event or a cause of rupture but a continuing quest for rationality. He recognizes Muslims as *dayee* (those who have been given the responsibility to invite others to Allah and the truth), non-Muslims as *mad'u* (those who are called to by Muslims). Khan argues that in their capacity as dayees, Muslims have to tolerate the oppression and injustice of other nations. In his opinion, without this tolerance, 'that atmosphere cannot be produced which is required for the effective performance of da'wa'.[24] From our point of view, this evocation of the rational spirit of people of all faiths, in Khan's project of dawat, represents a clear adherence to the constitutional expression of the freedom of religion, in which conversion is always understood as a rational choice.

Dawat-e-Islam: Faith and/or a right

A very different version of Dawat-e-Islam is offered by Maulana Ali Mian Nadwi. His dawat project is more concerned with specificity of particular social and political context and the purity of argument.[25] He argues that the methods of inviting people towards the message of Allah are contingent upon the sociocultural formation of society. Therefore, there are no 'fixed rules and regulations' for Dawat-e-Islam.[26] This context-sensitive mode of Dawat-e-Islam is supplemented by two other necessary components—linguistic clarity and purity of intention. Nadwi writes, 'Linguistic competence is of the utmost importance for the purpose of da'wa [. . .] And the most important ingredient is sincerity and an earnest urge to persuade others.'[27]

Nadwi also talk about the strength of Dawat-e-Islam. In his opinion, 'The powerful nations like USA or Soviet Russia will never be able to win the hearts of people as Islam has won them. The call of true Islamic faith which draws hearts of Muslims unfailingly is like a magnet that pulls iron chips towards it. Nothing in the world but faith (iman) has such a power.'[28] Nadwi, however, does not elaborate on the crucial relationship between the propagation of Islamic ideas and the conversion of non-Muslims as the final outcome, especially in the Indian context. To understand this slight vagueness in Nadwi's explanation, we have to pay attention to his understanding of politics.

It is important to remember that despite his initial critique of politics, Nadwi emerged as a key figure in the debates on Muslim personal law and, later, on the Babri Masjid–Ram temple dispute.[29] His take on overtly political issues helps him in offering a very clear perspective on the expected role of the state, especially with regard to religious and cultural minorities. Nadwi asserts, 'If minorities exist in the country, then safeguarding and keeping secure their religions, their places of worship, their personal laws and [. . .] language [. . .] is necessary [. . .] This is the primary duty of every government and no government [. . .] deserves to be called a government [. . .] if it cannot provide it.'[30] This important observation not only demonstrates Nadwi's political activism but also underlines his understanding of Dawat-e-Islam in a secular–constitutional context.

In his book *Muslims in India* (1960/1976), Nadwi argues that Islam did not come to India to destroy Hinduism. In contrast, Muslim preachers and saints brought Islam with the message of love. He claims that Muslims recognized India as their motherland and established great empires.[31] This Muslim contribution played a pivotal role in the cultural advancement of Indian civilization. He writes:

> They (Muslims) brought with them to India a new, practical and highly rationalistic religion, mature knowledge, a progressive culture and an evolved civilization which included within it all that was best in the cultural stock of many nations—it represented a synthesis of the natural wholesomeness of the Arab disposition.[32]

According to Nadwi, Muslims rediscovered the ancient sciences and philosophy of India and introduced it to the wider world. On the basis of this historical contribution of Islam, Nadwi proposes a slightly milder critique of the state. Describing the unjust and partial system of education, the decline of Urdu and other socio-economic issues related to Indian Muslims, Nadwi questioned state policies. He asserts: 'Muslims are not only citizens of an equal status with anybody in India; they are among its chief builders and architects, and hold [a] position second to none among the people of the world for selfless service to the motherland.'[33]

This historically embedded argument introduces us to a rather nuanced meaning of Islamic dawat. Nadwi's framework is not only about preparing Muslims to introduce Islam to non-Muslims but also about making them aware of their constitutionally granted rights. He traces compatibility between Islamic principles and democratic norms to conceptualize the Muslims of India as an identifiable minority community—which has a distinct culture and religion. The purpose of dawat, in this case, is to spread the message of this distinctiveness to Muslims, non-Muslims and, above all, to the state.[34]

Dawat as provocation

Zakir Naik's dawat project is new in two senses: it is new because it began only in the 1990s and somehow made him one of the most visible Muslim religious faces—online and offline! It is also new because unlike other postcolonial Sunni da'wa movements, Naik makes a direct appeal to evoke the Quran and Hadith for inviting, primarily, the non-Muslims. For him, 'Da'wah means a "call" or "invitation" [. . .] to invite non-Muslims to Islam as well as Muslims to the true understanding and practice of Islam.'[35] In this sense, Naik is critical of the reformist work of the Tablighi Jamaat kind. He says, 'Many Muslims [. . .] doing *islaah* (reform) have completely ignored Da'wah [. . .] Therefore, it is [. . .] our responsibility to concentrate on Da'wah in order to fill this vacuum.'[36]

Two important features of this direct dawat project are relevant—Naik's provocative rejection of other religious traditions and his adherence to original sources to find out the true meanings of Islam. Replying to a question regarding the use of term 'kafir' for non-Muslims, Naik says: 'Kafir is derived from the word *kufr*, which means one who conceals [. . .] the truth of Islam [. . .] If any non-Muslim considers the word kafir as an abuse, he may choose to accept Islam and then we will stop referring to him [as] a kafir.' Similarly, when he is asked about the freedom of religion in Islamic regimes, he argues that since Islam is the only true religion, and Muslims believe in it, the propagation of other religions is not permissible in an Islamic country. By the same logic, Naik also supports the entry restriction imposed on non-Muslims in the cities of Mecca and Medina. He says, 'The primary condition required for any human being to enter Makkah or Medina is to say [. . .] there is no God but Allah and Muhammad (PBUH) is his messenger.'[37]

The 'go back to the original' is the second aspect of his dawat project. Naik claims that the most appropriate method of understanding Islam is to 'understand the authentic sources of Islam—the Qur'an and the authentic hadith'. In his opinion, the Quran, being the words of Allah, could only be decoded through the sayings of Prophet Muhammad because it was revealed to him. Evoking this text-centric approach, Naik seems to rule out all possibility of human intervention in the divinity of Islam. For him, the words of Allah as well as the meanings given to these words by the Prophet are fixed, objective, unbiased and, above all, rational.

This strict adherence to Quranic textuality helps Naik gain legitimacy for his explanations. He does not recognize the Hindu gods Rama and Krishna as prophets of Allah as he does not find their names in the Quran and the Hadith; he opposes customary practices such as wearing a *mangalsutra* by Muslim women (a thread worn by married women, mainly Hindus in India) because he finds it offensive to the Islamic dress code; he does not approve of music because there is no mention of it in the texts.

As a product of new media—the TV, the Internet and the mobile phone—Naik recognizes a new religious audience, namely, migrated Muslim communities living in the West and the Middle East, in Asia and the generations of South Asian Muslims whose religiosity does not disapprove of television and the Internet. These communities, which experience very different trajectories of modern life, actually become the inseparable components of what might be called an online umma (community). From our point of view, the structure of this online umma is very significant—it is not merely constituted at a point when Naik delivers his speeches in front of a large congregation; rather, it is also formed, in fact, more powerfully, when the images of this Islamic public attending Naik's programmes are disseminated through the Internet and mobile apps. Naik, in this sense, addresses a community that follows his image—that of a skull-capped (this cap has become a Muslim cap in recent years!), well-clad (he always wears official suits), English-educated Muslim doctor, who relies primarily on his exceptional memory and scientific knowledge!

Naik's Dawat-e-Islam project is criticized for being highly provocative. It is described as 'tempered jihad' because of its seemingly sympathetic attitude toward Islamic fundamentalism. Naik, interestingly, does not find this allegation problematic. Instead, he argues, 'A fundamentalist is a person who follows and adheres to the doctrine or theory he is following.'[38] He describes himself as well as all practising Muslims as fundamentalist! The same logic is evoked to justify terrorism. Naik argues that 'a true Muslim should be a terrorist to selective people, i.e., anti-social elements, and not to the common innocent people.'[39] These refined commonsense explanations somehow contribute to Naik's image of a prominent Muslim figure, who is usually found in the top ranks of various lists of 'influential individuals.'

Naik's deviation from the dominant postcolonial Dawat-e-Islam movements is not surprising. His ideas do not stem from the minority rights-centric Indian discourse of law. As a result, the thin dividing line between propagation and conversion is clearly disregarded by him to offer rather polemical, straight and ready-to-use Islamic responses. This straightforwardness, however, does not work in recent years, when Naik's NGO and TV channels have been closed by the government and access to his website restricted. Responding to these actions, Naik, probably for the first time, evokes the legal–constitutional discourse. He says:

> The system and agencies have been used to suit a pre-meditated result set by the government of India, a government that took an oath to uphold the Indian Constitution, the same Constitution that allows me the freedom to profess, practise, and propagate my religion. Let us not be gullible to think this was just an attack on me. It is an attack on whom I represent, the Indian Muslims. It is an attack on *peace, democracy and justice* [. . .] India is my home, my roots, and I will fight this ban come what may.[40]

A *legalized* Islam?

Our discussion shows that law and constitutional values function as influential factors that determine the various representations of Islam as a religion in India. However, this explicit adherence to constitutionalism by Islamic religious scholars should not merely be read as a success story of an India-specific secularism. Scholars like Ali Mian Nadwi and Wahiduddin Khan do not simply celebrate the discourse of minority rights; instead, they engage with it, interpret it and offer new and creative articulations of Dawat-e-Islam. This acceptability of secular law does not prevent them from speaking of the supremacy of Islam as a religion in India, of the contributions of Muslims in the past and, above all, from envisaging a world where Islam ultimately rules.

Our discussion shows that Tablighi Jamaat's expressed commitment to apolitical dawat of Islam functions within the broad framework of the law. The agenda of preparing Muslims for deen never poses any challenge to secular law and allows the Jamaat to operate in a closed sphere of religion. JIH, on the contrary, seems to identify the debate on 'propagation versus conversion' as a vantage point to reinterpret the project of dawat. This strategy has helped them to disseminate their version of Islam in postcolonial India. Similarly, Wahiduddin Khan's emphasis on modern rationality offers him an opportunity to represent dawat as a rational interpretation of Islam, which he finds compatible with Indian secularism. For Ali Mian, law and secularism have been deeply ingrained in the social values of Muslims. He argues that reasserting Islamic sovereignty in the postcolonial period is a legitimate constitutional right. Zakir Naik is the only Islamic preacher who frequently crosses the propagation versus conversion line. His image-centric identity makes it possible for him to talk of the conversion of non-Muslims more directly on TV shows. However, this attitude changes radically when Naik's conversion-centric Dawat-e-Islam is interrogated by Indian authorities. Naik, like other postcolonial Indian Islamic scholars, evokes the discourse of minority rights and asserts his Indian identity to justify his Islamic adherence.

This brings us to the main argument of this chapter. I argue that postcolonial Islamic discourse in India is highly multilayered. It functions like a pendulum. The ideal textual interpretations of Islam and the concept of Islamic supremacy are at one extreme end of the pendulum's swing, while the legal–constitutional considerations and assertion of minority rights are at the other end.

4

Why Does Hindutva Need Muslims?

Why Muslims?

Mohan Bhagwat, the Sarsanghchalak of the RSS, delivered a series of lectures on the ideas and ideology of the RSS in September 2018. In an attempt to offer an acceptable and inclusive meaning of the term 'Hindutva', Bhagwat makes the following observations:

That very set of values are christened as Hindutva. It stands for unity in diversity, reconciliation, sacrifice, temperance, gratitude. The truth that lies at its crux is discovered here, in our realm.[1]

[. . .]

The collective notion of values belonging to the religions that are sprung from the entirety, that is India, is known as Hindutva [. . .] Therefore, the idea which we call as Hindutva is synonymous with the notion of patriotism, the other constituent of it, which is born out of the culture of that very precept of values. This is the mark of India. And, India belongs to that.[2]

[. . .]

This ideology is our continuum, which [the] world recognizes as Hindutva. We, therefore, claim that ours is a Hindu Nation.[3]

[. . .]

According to us, Hindutva has three basics. Patriotism, glory of our forebears, and culture.[4]

[. . .]

It can never be construed [as] the undesirability of Muslims in its ambit. If ever it is claimed that it does not desire Muslims in its ambit, that day it will die down as Hindutva.[5]

Bhagwat was not reading from a written text (the transcriptions of the speeches were later uploaded on the RSS website). These points came out as 'references' in his long speeches. Although one may find them scattered, repetitive and unrelated, these observations could be systematized to find out a workable conceptualization of what Bhagwat calls Hindutva.

He seems to suggest:

(a) *India-specific values*: There are five core values (unity in diversity, coordination, sacrifice, tolerance, thankfulness), which are common to all those sects and sub-sects which originated in India.

(b) *India means territory*: India can only be understood as a geographic territory. Therefore, only those ideas and sects which have emerged within these geographic boundaries may justifiably be described as Indian sects.

(c) *Naming:* Since the ideology of all 'Indian' sects is known as Hindutva throughout the world, it is reasonable to identify India as a Hindu Rashtra.

(d) *Core beliefs:* Hindutva has three foundational beliefs—patriotism, ancestral pride and culture. Therefore, it is appropriate to expect everyone who lives in India to submit to these core values.

(e) *Muslims*: Muslims are important for the survival of Hindutva.

On the third day of the programme, Bhagwat elaborated his ideas during the question–answer sessions and provided a sequence to his thoughts. (Incidentally, it was not an unusual interactive session. The invited audience submitted written questions and Bhagwat responded to them thematically!) Replying to a set of questions related to the RSS's position on minorities and the growing isolation of Muslims, he said:

किस आधार पर हम आपको अपना नहीं माने वह पंथ संप्रदाय नहीं है भाषा नहीं है जाति नहीं है कुछ नहीं है। मातृभूमि, संस्कृति, पूर्वज ये है। उन पर हम जोर देते हैं। उसको हम अपनी राष्ट्रीयता के घटक मानते हैं।[6]

This statement makes it clear that Bhagwat's so-called inclusive Hindutva, which has also been seen as a revisionist version of the RSS, does not deviate from the old language of 'you Muslims and we Hindus'. He seems to employ the three core beliefs of his version of Hindutva to remind Muslims that they have to come forward and prove their nationalism.

In this sense, the motherland in territorial terms may also be read as a warning to Muslims that they must recognize India as their true homeland! The Hindutva adherence to 'purity of culture' may be seen as a reminder that Muslims must stick to the five core values of Indian/Hindutva sects. And unquestioned submission to ancestral pride is a strict advice to Muslims, making it clear that they must give priority to their Indian ancestors over their pan-Islamic connections.

Yet, this reformulation of Hindutva's three core beliefs does not fully explain Bhagwat's enigmatic comment that Hindutva without Muslims is meaningless. Was it just a passing reference or a *jumla*? Why does Hindutva need Muslims? This is precisely what this chapter asks. It explores the changing meanings of the term Hindutva, and tries to situate Muslims in it. More specifically, it looks at two related questions: (a) If the three core beliefs of Hindutva are universally applicable to all those who reside in contemporary India, then why is that only Muslims are asked to prove their submission to the motherland? And even if this demand is accepted and (b) What could be the criteria to evaluate their patriotism?

Versions of Hindutva

The BJP's senior leader and former chief minister of Himachal Pradesh Shanta Kumar made an interesting comment in July 2018. He said:

> Hindutva is being misunderstood. And our own people are responsible for this misunderstanding [. . .] I have raised it within the party [. . .] Hindutva is what Vivekananda said [. . .] If somebody fights over it, he is not a Hindu [. . .] some mistakes are made by our own people [. . .] This is not the Hindutva the BJP swears by.[7]

Shanta Kumar's observation is not surprising. For a long time, the RSS, the Bharatiya Jana Sangh (BJS) and even the BJP did not recognize Hindutva as a relevant cultural or political concept. The complicated story of Hindutva actually goes against the popular portrayal of this term as a unified set of cultural political principles. It is marked by a number of contradictions and contestation. Therefore, the changing meanings of Hindutva, especially with regard to Muslims, must be traced historically.

The term 'Hindutva' was coined by V.D. Savarkar, the leader of the Hindu Mahasabha, in 1923. In his book *Hindutva*, Savarkar identifies a few characteristics of the Hind nation—a marked geography, a common language, a common culture and a belief that this land is a holy land. He argues:

> A Hindu [. . .] is he who looks upon the land that extends from Sindu to Sindu—from the Indus to the Seas, as the land of his

forefathers—his Fatherland (Pitribhu), who inherits the blood of that race whose first discernible source could be traced to the Vedic Saptasindhus [. . .] who has inherited [. . .] the common classical language Sanskrit and is represented by a common history, a common literature, art and architecture, law and jurisprudence, rites and rituals, ceremonies and sacraments, fairs and festivals; and who above all, addresses this land, this Sindhusthan as his Holyland (Punyabhu), as the land of his prophets and seers, of his godmen and gurus, the land of piety and pilgrimage.[8]

This European nation state–style definition of Hindutva is full of contradictions. Savarkar not only excludes Muslims and Christians from his imagination of Hindu society (as their Holyland is outside India!) but he also disregards the cultures and languages of those communities who do not wish to inherit Sanskrit as a source of identity. In fact, there is no space for cultural distinctiveness, democratic dissent and federal values—the principles, which are defended by the Indian Constitution—in Savarkar's schema of Hindutva state.

The RSS did not accept Savarakar's conceptualization of Hindutva (although his ideas continue to inspire their political rhetoric even in the 1940s). In his book *Bunch of Thoughts*, former RSS chief and one of the main ideologues of the Sangh M.S. Golwalkar rejects this overemphasis on the term Hindutva. Quoting Dr Hedgewar (the founder of the RSS), Golwalkar argues that even the term 'Hindu' is not appropriate to describe the mission of Sangh. He notes:

Doctorji used to say that in our land the word 'Rashtriya' naturally means 'Hindu' and therefore the word 'Hindu' need not be used. He would say, 'If we use the word 'Hindu', it will only mean that we consider ourselves only as one of the innumerable communities in this land and that we do not realize our natural status as the nationals of this country.' (p. 116)[9]

For Golwalkar and the RSS, at least in the 1960s, the term Hindutva was a communal expression. This was the reason why in all the resolutions passed by the RSS in the period 1950–91, the term 'Bhartiyakarn' (Indianization) was used very prominently. In fact, Golwalkar compares the Hindu Mahasabha and Savarkar with the Muslim League! He says:

> Veer Savarkarji wrote a beautiful book *Hindutva* and [the] Hindu Mahasabha based itself on that pure philosophy of Hindu nationalism. But once the Hindu Mahasabha passed a resolution that Congress should not give up its 'nationalist' stand by holding talks with [the] Muslim League but should ask [the] Hindu Mahasabha to do that job! It only means that [. . .] Hindu Mahasabha represented the Hindu counterpart of the rabidly communal, anti-national Muslim League![10]

It is important to mention that the RSS still upholds this criticism. In a recent article, Rakesh Sinha, an official thinker (*vicharak*) of Sangh and a nominated member of the Rajya Sabha, makes a very similar point. Quoting the above-mentioned passage, Sinha points out: 'No literature of the RSS advocates discrimination against minorities or the formation of a theocratic state. Critics intentionally impose the Hindu Mahasabha's perspective on the RSS.'[11]

Does it mean that the RSS's Hindutva is different from Savarkar's Hindutva?

The term Hindutva is wholeheartedly accepted by the RSS as a slogan during the heyday of the Babri Masjid–Ram Mandir debate in the late 1980s. However, it was only in 1996 that Hindutva was eventually recognized as an ideological entity. Two interesting examples are relevant here.

On 18 January 1996, the Vishwa Hindu Parishad, an organization created by the RSS in 1964, passed a resolution called the Hindu Agenda. The first point of this resolution defines Hindutva thus:

Hindutva is synonymous with nationality and Hindu society is undisputedly the mainstream of Bharat. Hindu interest is the national interest. Hence, the honour of Hindutva and Hindu interests should be protected at all cost[s].[12]

The enthusiasm to appropriate Hindutva as an ideological phenomenon can also be found in the self-description of the RSS. According to the RSS's official website:

Not only the context of Bharat, but also the global situation re-confirms the validity of the philosophical foundation of [the] Rashtriya Swayamsevak Sangh. That the coming or twenty-first century will be a century dominated by Hindutva and what it stands for is a prophecy which has been heard from many quarters, including eminent historians.[13]

It is clear that Hindutva is celebrated by the RSS, but there is no serious effort to define it. This confusion is also very evident in the BJP's stated political ideology.

The 1998 manifesto of the BJP describes it as a party which is deeply committed to the idea of Hindutva, a political philosophy that is supposed to be a religion-neutral term.[14] According to the national website of the BJP:

The BJP is committed to the concept of 'One Nation, One People and One Culture' [. . .] The unique cultural and social diversity in India is woven into a larger civilizational fabric by thousands of years of common living and common and shared values, beliefs, customs, struggles, joy and sorrow, as well as symbols of high degree of unity without uniformity [. . .] This cultural heritage which is central to all regions, religions and languages, is a civilizational identity and constitutes the cultural nationalism of India which is the core of Hindutva. This we believe is the identity of our ancient nation 'Bharatvarsha'. [15]

However, this commitment to Hindutva is not part of the official constitution of the party. Article IV of the BJP constitution, published in 2012, says:

The Party shall be committed to nationalism and national integration, democracy, 'Gandhian approach to socio-economic issues, leading to the establishment of an egalitarian society free from exploitation', positive secularism, that is 'sarv dharm sambhav', and value-based politics.[16]

Hindutva is not the official philosophy of the BJP either. The BJP website describes 'Integral Humanism' as the stated philosophy of the party. Integral humanism is based on the four lectures delivered by Deen Dayal Upadhyaya in the mid-1960s. These lectures offer a critique of national politics by evoking the intrinsic relationship between individual and society.

Interestingly, there are two official versions of the Deen Dayal Upadhyay lectures. The contents of the lectures given on the national website of the BJP are very different from that on the Gujarat BJP official website.

The national website's version of Lecture 3 ('Individual of Society') talks about the specificities of 'group feelings' and group identity. It says:

[The] Group has its feelings too. These are not exactly similar to the individual's feelings. Group feelings cannot be considered a mere arithmetic addition of individual feelings [. . .] A person may be ready to forgive and forget a personal abuse to him, but the same man loses his temper if you abuse his society. It is possible that a person who is of high character in his personal life is unscrupulous as a member of the society. Similarly, an individual can be good in society but not so in his individual life.[17]

This description is concluded with an explanatory paragraph.

There is a thesis is that when a group of people live together for a long time, by historical tradition and association, by continued intercourse, they begin to think similarly and have similar customs. It is true that some uniformity is brought about by staying together.[18]

But this is not the case with the BJP's Gujarat website. Between the above-mentioned two paragraphs, there is an explicatory description, which says:

Let me give you an illustration. Once, during a conversation between Shri Vinobaji and the Sarsanghchalak of Rashtriya Swayamsevak Sangh, Shri Guruji, a question arose as to where the modes of thinking of Hindus and Muslims differ. Guruji said to Vinobaji that there are good and bad people in every society. There can be found honest and good people in Hindus as well as in Muslims. Similarly, rascals can be seen in both the societies. No particular society has a monopoly of goodness. However, *it is observed that Hindus, even if they are rascals in individual life, when they come together in a group, they always think of good things. On the other hand, when two Muslims come together, they propose and approve of things which they themselves in their individual capacity would not even think of. They start thinking in an altogether different way.* This is an everyday experience. Vinobaji admitted that there was truth in this observation but had no reasons to explain it. If we analyse this situation, we shall discover that the modes of thinking of an individual and of a society are always different. These two do not bear an arithmetic relation. *If a thousand good men gather together, it cannot be said for certain that they will think similarly of good things.*[19]

So the question is which 'integral humanism' is authentic? Does the BJP as a registered political party still believe that Muslims as a group cannot think of 'good things'? What is the relationship between integral humanism and Hindutva?

The RSS and the BJP's strategy to justify their Hindutva by referring to the 1996 Supreme Court judgement (the famous Bal Thackeray case in which Hindutva was defined as 'a way of life') is also problematic. It is true that the court used the expression 'way of life' for recognizing Hindutva; yet, it asks all the political parties and other stakeholders to stop using religion for political benefits. The court defines Hindutva as a synonym of Hinduism and makes a clear distinction between Hindutva and political mobilization in the name of religion. The court observes:

The term 'Hindutva' is related more to the way of life of the people in the subcontinent. It is difficult to appreciate how [. . .] the term 'Hindutva' or 'Hinduism' per se [. . .] can be assumed to mean and be equated with narrow fundamentalist Hindu religious bigotry.[20]

In the concluding part of the judgement, it is forcefully argued that:

Fundamentalism of any colour or kind must be curbed with a heavy hand to preserve and promote the secular creed of the nation. Any misuse of these terms must, therefore, be dealt with strictly [. . .] Our conclusion is that [. . .] three speeches of Bal Thackeray amount to corrupt practice [. . .] Since the appeal made to the voters in these speeches was to vote for Dr Ramesh Prabhoo on the ground[s] of his religion as a Hindu.

Ironically, the BJP as well as the opponents of the BJP completely ignored this concluding part of the Supreme Court judgement. The BJP began to use Hindutva as a political concept, ignoring the legal–ethical warning inherent in the judgement, while the secularists denounced Hindutva ignoring the positive meanings of it offered by the court.

This is exactly what Justice J.S. Verma, who delivered this famous judgement, outlined in an interview in 2003. He said, 'The politicians who are practising or using Hindutva to their advantage are misconstruing and misusing it. They have not fully appreciated the abstract of the judgement.'[21] This observation is absolutely correct. The opponent of the BJP legitimized the BJP/RSS's ambiguous and selective use of the term Hindutva. They created a binary between Hindutva and secularism as if Hindutva can only be understood as an antithesis of their version of secularism!

Nevertheless, the success of the BJP in 2014 created an intellectual pressure on the RSS to offer a systematic interpretation of Hindutva. Bhagwat's lectures are the very first attempt by the RSS to define what they mean by it. At the same time, the opponents of the BJP/RSS are also struggling to work out a non-BJP/RSS version of political Hinduism, if not Hindutva. Interestingly, the struggle to define Hindutva always revolves around Muslims!

Hindutva's Muslims

Opposing the recommendations of the *Sachar Committee Report*, Mohan Bhagwat argued that Muslims in India must realize that their forefathers were Hindus, who eventually converted to Islam.[22] Bhagwat has been making comments of this kind for a long time. There is no doubt that the majority of South Asian Muslims are converted Muslims. (By this logic, except Prophet Muhammad, all Muslims of the world are converted, as their forefathers embraced Islam at different historical moments!) However, the connection Bhagwat establishes between converted Muslims and the Sachar report is highly misleading. Does it mean that Muslims are marginalized because they are converted? Or, does it mean that 'ghar wapsi' (the reconversion of the converted Muslims) would be the ultimate way out to deal with the economic, cultural and educational backwardness of Muslims?

Bhagwat's comment is not entirely new. Savarkar, too, in his 1923 book *Hindutva* talks of converted Muslims and Christians. In his opinion, even converted Muslims cannot be accommodated into the Hindutva fold. He says:

> Some of our Mohammedan or Christian countrymen who had originally been forcibly converted to a non-Hindu religion and who consequently have inherited along with Hindus, a common Fatherland and a greater part of the wealth of a common culture—language, law, customs, folklore and history—are not and cannot be recognized as Hindus. For though Hinduism to them is Fatherland as [it is] to any other Hindu, yet, it is not to them a Holyland [. . .] Their Holyland is far off in Arabia or Palestine.[23]

There is an inherent contradiction in Savarkar's argument. In his opinion, the Hindu religion should not be treated as the decisive criterion to determine the Hindutva of any group of people; however, when it comes to converted Muslims and Christians, their belief in holy places of worship is treated as a principle to evaluate their patriotism. Savarkar, interestingly, evades this inconsistency in this small book.

Despite the fact that M.S. Golwalkar was very critical of Savarkar and his conception of Hindutva, he adheres to Savarkar's framework. In his view, Muslims, Christians and communists are the three main internal threats that India faces. According to him:

> Muslims must realize that we are all one people and it is the same blood that courses in our veins [. . .] they are only Hindu converts [. . .] the problem can and must be solved by Indian Muslims owning the country and its ancient culture as theirs.[24]

The converted Muslims are seen here as Hindus by blood. But Golwalkar, like Savarkar, does not believe that the 'pure Hindu blood' criterion would be able to solve the problem. In his opinion, converted Muslims, like the other 'racial' Muslims, must prove their loyalty towards Hindus and India.

This formulation is self-contradictory in two senses: (a) If converted Muslims are actually the 'poor Hindu victims of forcible conversion', why should they be subject to any 'loyalty test'? (b) Is the natural 'purity of Hindu blood' not capable of erasing the impact of ideas such as Islam even now?

The BJS, the predecessor of the BJP, however, offered a practical way out to this 'Muslim question'. The party's official manifesto of 1951 says:

> Jana Sangh considers them (Muslims) flesh of our flesh, the blood of our blood [. . .] It looks forward to their disassociating foreign ways from the tenets of their religion. They are welcome to worship the Islamic way. They are expected to live the Bharatiya way.[25]

This emphasis on the Bharatiya way eventually led to a full-fledged idea of Indianization. The 1957 manifesto of the BJS, for example, identifies Indianization as one of the main objectives. It says:

> For the preservation of national unity [. . .] Jana Sangh will take the following steps: (a) Creating a feeling of equality and oneness of Hindu society by liquidating untouchability and casteism (b) Nationalizing all non-Hindus by inculcating in them the ideal of Bharatiya culture.[26]

It is clear that Savarkar, Golwalkar, the BJS and even Bhagwat make a clear distinction between Hindus and non-Hindus. A born Hindu, in this framework, would naturally qualify as a patriot, while non-Hindus would have to be Indianized (read Hinduized!).

Let us recapitulate the discussion by outlining the Hindutva imagination of the Muslims of India.

- *Types of Muslims*: There are two kinds of Muslims in India—the foreigners (or racial), whose forefathers came from outside the territory called India, and the local Hindus, who were forcibly converted to Islam by the Muslim rulers.
- *Nature of Islamic ideas*: Islam is the antithesis of Hindutva. Since it did not originate in the territory of India, it cannot be called 'Indian'. The oneness of God does not allow Muslims to appreciate/imbibe Hindutva's openness and religious plurality.
- *Influence of Islam*: Islamic ideas influence both types of Muslims and encourage separatist tendencies. The partition of India strengthened this tendency.
- *Hindutva's way out*: Muslims should not change their mode of worship, but they should adhere to the core Indian/Hindutva values.

What should Muslims do to become truly Indian?

Who are you—a Muslim or an Indian? This has been the most dominant and straightforward question for Muslims in postcolonial India. Interestingly, this abstract question has been translated in a number of different ways over the years. I have divided these questions into five categories to make sense of the term Indianization. A few examples:

The Indianization of Islam

- Why do you worship facing the Kaaba as it is outside India?
- Why don't you visit Hindu temples as many Hindus visit shrines and dargahs?
- Why don't you stop azan as it disturbs Hindus?
- Why do you need mosques when you can offer namaz anywhere?
- Why do you offer namaz on roads as it disturbs the traffic?
- Why do you need graveyards as there is a shortage of land?
- Why don't you remove a few verses of the Quran as these verses are anti-national in nature?
- Why don't give up claims over historic mosques as most of the mosques were built by Muslim rulers by destroying temples?

The Indianization of Muslim everyday life

- Why don't you say 'Vande Mataram'?
- Why don't you say 'Bharat Mata ki Jai'?
- Why don't you come to celebrate Hindu festivals as these constitute Indian culture?
- Why do you come to celebrate Hindu festivals—to lure Hindu girls?
- Why do you celebrate the victory of Pakistan in a cricket match against India?

- Why don't you have Indian Hindu/Sanskrit names for your children?

The Indianization of Muslim family life

- Why do you marry four times?
- Why don't you use contraceptives?
- Why do Muslim men marry Hindu women?
- Why don't you appreciate a wedding between a Hindu man and a Muslim woman?

The Indianization of Muslim eating habits

- Why don't you stop killing/eating the cow as it's a sacred animal for us?
- Why don't you give up eating meat as it hurts the sentiments of vegetarian Hindus/Indians?
- Why do you take pride in foreign dishes such as biryani?
- Why do you want Islamic religious schools as it goes against the fundamental ethos of this land?

The Indianization of Muslim politics

- Why do you want Muslim personal law?
- Why do you want to be called a 'minority'?
- Why don't you oppose Islamic terrorism and Pakistan's involvement in Kashmir?
- Why do you want the protection of Urdu—when it's not an Indian language?
- Why don't you give up your claim over the Babri Masjid as it's a sentimental issue for Hindus?
- Why do you want reservation as it is only meant for reforming Hindu society?

This list will always remain incomplete because it is based on an inherent contradiction between Indian Muslims and the various conceptions of Hindutva. Even if all Muslims start singing 'Vande Mataram' wholeheartedly, change their names, remove a few verses from the Quran, they won't become a Hindu/Indian/patriot, as there is a strong apprehension about the process of Indianization itself! Indianization cannot change the blood and cannot reverse the historical tragedy called conversion!

Let me come back to the main question: Why does Hindutva need Muslims? The core of Hindutva of all kinds is based on historically constituted, anti-Muslim rhetoric. Hindutva ideologues offer a subjugated imagination of the medieval Indian past as a 'historic rupture'. This pessimistic Hindu history is used to celebrate the courage of a few selective Hindu heroes such as Shivaji and Maharana Pratap to denounce Muslim rulers, especially Aurangzeb and Akbar. The Hindus of independent India are called upon to erase this historical injustice by asserting their anti-Muslim Hinduness.

The Muslims of India are important for the survival of this political imagination for two reasons. First of all, they could be shown as the children of those who once humiliated and defeated the Hindus. The rhetorical expressions for Muslims, such as 'Babar ki aulad' (progeny of Babar), emerge out of this Hindutva anxiety. Since it is not possible to get rid of Muslims completely, it is easier for Hindutva to make them a permanent 'other'.

Secondly, the evocation of Muslim identity also helps Hindutva hide its ambiguities and internal contradictions. The RSS's criticism of Hindutva in the 1960s and its wholehearted appropriation of it in the 1990s survives because of its conventional anti-Muslim position. Similarly, the BJP's unclear position on its stated political philosophy—integral humanism—could not become a political issue in the wake of the party's so-called submission to the ideology of Hindutva even without recognizing it as a fundamental ideological tenant.

Yes, Bhagwat is right. Hindutva without Muslims is meaningless!

Source: Vikram Nayak.

PART II

UNPACKING SIYASI MUSLIMS

5

Muslims as a Minority

Muslim affairs versus minority affairs

In her short-lived career as minister for minority affairs, Najma Heptulla made three very strong arguments about the status of Muslims as a minority.

Immediately after taking charge of the ministry, she clarified that Muslim affairs should not be confused with the issues and concerns of the 'minorities'. She said: 'This is not the ministry for Muslim affairs, this is the ministry of Minority affairs [. . .] Muslims are not minorities. Parsis are. We have to see how we can help them so that their numbers do not diminish.'[1]

Her second argument was related to the growing alienation of Muslims after 2014. Heptulla argued that Muslim alienation had always been an issue in India. Accusing the Congress of vote-bank politics, Heptulla said, 'It is not that today Muslims are feeling alienated. Muslims have been feeling alienated since Independence, because they have been relegated to such [a] backward situation.'[2]

Heputlla's third argument was about Muslim reservation. She said, 'This government is not making promises, it's doing the work. It's making Muslims capable enough to do something for themselves and not depend on this reservation. And reservation on the basis of religion is totally wrong and it should not happen.'[3]

These three comments certainly go against the so-called secular political correctness that was established during the UPA 1 and UPA 2 periods. Although it is true that Najma Heptulla followed the party line and did not deviate from the unspoken stand of the BJP on Muslim isolation, there is an element of truth in her observations.

Her distinction between two related terms, 'Muslims' and 'minority', is absolutely valid. 'Muslim' as a religious community as well as a census category is technically different from the constitutional term 'minority'. The argument that Muslim marginalization is a postcolonial Indian phenomenon created and nurtured by the Congress elite is politically justifiable. And her assertion that reservation on the basis religion is unlawful is also technically correct.

Yet, the manner in which Muslims are described as a minority, even by Heptulla, is problematic.

There is a positive portrayal of their minority status, which celebrates the triumph of Indian secularism. The protection of Muslims' religious and culture rights are often evoked to underline the success of the 'unity in diversity' thesis.

However, there is an equally powerful negative depiction of Muslims as a minority. It is argued that minority rights given to Muslims go against the principle of equality. The minority status of Muslims, it is alleged, legitimizes the politics of appeasement and encourages separatist tendencies.

This oversimplified formulation raises two sets of issues.

The first set of questions is technical in nature, such as asking what is the legal–constitutional meaning of the term 'minority'? And what is the criterion to identify a minority?

The second set of issues is political. If Muslims are seen as a national minority, shall we call the Hindus of India a 'national majority'? And, for that reason, is it legitimate to interpret the recognition of Muslim distinctiveness as a form of political appeasement? This is what this chapter aims to discuss.

Undefined minorities and Muslims

It is worth noting that the minority–majority in colonial India were always recognized as permanent entities, especially on a religious basis. Hence, Hindus as the majority and Muslims and other non-Hindu groups as minorities were recognized as the legitimate stakeholders. This communalization of the minority–majority eventually led to the Partition.

Recognizing this deeply ingrained communal impulse, the Constituent Assembly of India worked out a highly undefined and fluid conception of a minority. The Constitution offers us two attributes of a minority group: the distinctiveness of a minority group in relation to majority culture (Articles 29–30), and the diversity of minorities, which means the recognition of various religious as well as linguistic communities as minorities (Articles 25, 26, 350).

The first feature of a minority categorically stresses upon the fact that a minority, being a numerical expression, cannot be attributed to any particular social group permanently. In this sense, Muslims, Sikhs and Christians 'become a minority' on a contextual basis. Even Hindus can be called a religious minority in Punjab, Kashmir and Nagaland.

The second constitutional feature suggests that apart from religion, language and culture should also be taken into consideration when defining a minority. That is the reason why we have constitutionally recognized linguistic and cultural minorities in India.

The distinction Nehru makes between the communalism of majority and the communalism of minority is very relevant here.

In the 1950s, the Nehru government enacted the Hindu Code Bill, but no such legislative initiatives were proposed to reform the Muslim personal law. Nehru was severely criticized for encouraging Muslim appeasement. In the open session of the All India Congress Committee, on 11 May 1958, Nehru responded to these criticisms. He said:

The communalism of the majority is far more dangerous than the communalism of the minority because it wears the garb of nationalism. We have thus communalism ingrained in us and it comes out quite quickly at the slightest provocation and even decent people begin to behave like barbarians when this communalism is aroused in them . . .' (Noorani 2003, 316)

This distinction between minority and majority communalism underlines Nehru's assertion that the distinctiveness of a minority is a constitutional commitment; hence, institutions should be able to deal with the anxieties and aspirations of minorities, which might take a communal overtone.

At the same time, Nehru also made another very important explanation. He sought to clarify the distinction between constitutional adherence to the unity and integrity of the Indian republic and the notion of Indianization—an idea that had been propagated by Hindu nationalists, mainly by the BJS in the 1950s.

This clarification had certain institutional manifestations as well. The Nehru government was keen to establish certain new forms of institutions to implement what was rhetorically known as 'unity in diversity'.

By the early 1960s, the idea of having a special institution to deal with the question of national integration emerged as a political necessity. The creation of the National Integration Council (NIC) in 1961 was the obvious outcome.

The official and stated objectives for which the NIC was constituted were not entirely related to the problems and anxieties of the religious minorities. The official statement of the National Integration Conference, 1961, defines national integration:

National integration is a psychological and educational process involving the development of a feeling of unity, solidarity and cohesion in the hearts of the people, a sense of common citizenship and a feeling of loyalty to the nation.[4]

Yet, the grievances of the minority were given a priority and it was suggested that the NIC 'should give early consideration to the setting up of machinery for the examination and redress of grievances of minorities'.

It is important to note here that the proceedings of the National Integration Conference, 1961, as well as agenda items discussed by the NIC focused primarily on the problems of integration with regard to linguistic minorities. The issues of religious minorities were discussed under the heading of 'communalism'!

This discussion brings us to two crucial technical points:

- Technically, any Indian community—religious as well as linguistic—may be identified as a minority on case-by-case basis. Muslims, thus, cannot technically be called a permanent minority in constitutional terms.
- Politically, however, the colonial discourse of minority/ majority as Hindu communalism versus Muslim separatism continued to survive in postcolonial India. Muslims were always addressed as a 'permanent minority' by the political elite, especially in the realm of competitive electoral politics.

Muslims and the Minorities Commission (1977–91)

In the 1977 elections, the Congress was defeated by the newly established Janata Party (JP) and the first non-Congress government at the Centre was established. The JP, which had evoked the 'persecution of minorities' as one of the main political arguments against Indira Gandhi's Emergency regime, established the Minorities Commission in 1978. In the official notification, it was noted:

> Despite the safeguards provided in the Constitution and the laws in force, there persists amongst the minorities a feeling of inequality and discrimination. In order to preserve secular traditions and to promote national integration, the Government of India attaches the highest importance to the enforcement of the safeguards provided for the minorities and is of the firm view that effective institutional arrangements are urgently required for the effective enforcement and implementation of all the safeguards provided for the minorities in the Constitution, in Central and state laws, and in government policies and administrative schemes enunciated from time to time [. . .] The Government [. . .] has [. . .] resolved to set up a Minorities Commission to safeguard the interests of minorities whether based on religion or language.[5]

To make sense of the status of this non-statutory entity called the Minorities Commission, we must understand the technical distinction between statutory bodies and non-statutory bodies.

A statutory body derives its powers from a law passed by the Parliament, while a non-statutory body comes into existence by an executive order. Statutory bodies are also different from institutional ones called 'constitutional bodies'. The constitutional bodies derive their authority from the

Constitution itself. In other words, constitutional bodies are formed by the Constitution which helps the government run properly.

The Minorities Commission, in this sense, was a non-statutory institution which came into existence through an official notification. It did not have the adequate legal weight to respond to the identifiable issues of minorities. Nevertheless, this commission was entrusted with the following functions:

(a) To evaluate the working of the various safeguards provided in the Constitution for the protection of minorities and in the laws passed by the Union and the state governments;

(b) To make recommendations with a view to ensuring the effective implementation and enforcement of all the safeguards and laws;

(c) To undertake a review of the implementation of the policies pursued by the Union and the state governments with respect to the minorities;

(d) To look into the specific complaints regarding the deprivation of the rights of and safeguards for the minorities;

(e) To conduct studies, research and analyses on the question of avoidance of discrimination against minorities;

(f) To suggest appropriate legal and welfare measures in respect of any minority;

(g) To serve as a National Clearance House for information in respect of the conditions of the minorities; and

(h) To make periodical reports at prescribed intervals to the government.[6]

The creation of the commission should also be seen in relation to the commissions constituted for the Scheduled Castes and Scheduled Tribes. It is worth noting that the National Commission for Scheduled Castes and the National Commission for

Scheduled Tribes were not created as two distinct constitutional bodies.

These commissions were initially established by the notification of the government in 1978. However, over the course of time, it evolved into a constitutional body. The Minorities Commission had a different trajectory. Despite a number of constitutional interventions, the commission could not attain constitutional status during the JP regime. A bill in this regard was tabled by the government in the Lok Sabha in 1978, which could not become a law and lapsed on two different occasions.

The establishment of the commission was also a political phenomenon. The opposition for such a body came from two very different ideological spectrums. The Congress opposed it precisely because it was the outcome of the politics of anti-Congressism that was nurtured and practised successfully by the JP.

The BJS, which was a constituent of the JP, was also uncomfortable with it. It was obviously going against the politics of the BJS, which had always evoked 'appeasement of minorities' as its core ideological position. L.K. Advani's speech in the Parliament in 1992 is a revealing example of this political anxiety. Opposing the National Commission for Minorities Bill, 1992, Advani said:

> I hold myself guilty for having been party to the creation of the Minorities Commission even though on an administrative level without any statutory back-up. I was in the Government [. . .] The manifesto of the Janata Party issued in 1977 spoke about a Civil Rights Commission, not about a Minorities Commission. That became an aberration, a distortion [. . .] Now this [passing an Act for the Commission in 1992] is being done by the Congress Party [. . .] I am sure that if the BJP had not been there in this strength, you would not have been satisfied with this kind

of statutory status. It is a relief that you are not able to give a constitutional status [. . .] This kind of Bill is addressed in name of course to the Christians, to the Parsis, to the Sikhs, etc., but actually it is addressed only to one section [. . .] You are going to commit a similar kind of monumental and historical blunder by passing this Bill.[7]

One can easily point out two kinds of anxieties here: technical and political. The Minorities Commission was just a non-statutory body in 1978 which was to be given the status of a statutory body in 1992. Despite this apparently weak status, it was seen as a problematic institution. In fact, it was presented as a distortion of the Civil Rights Commission.

Secondly, the creation of the Minorities Commission was interpreted as the political appeasement of religious minorities in general and Muslims in particular. It is worth noting that the commission did not make any attempt to 'define' the meaning of the term 'minority'. It relied on an unspecified expression, 'minority', to safeguard the interests of numerically inferior religious and linguistic groups. However, the political class offered concrete meaning to it.

Two important points come up here:

- Institutional moves (such as the Minorities Commission) to address the issues and concerns of those groups, who were designated as minorities, were always politicized as a Muslim-related initiative. The Muslim political elite also contributed to it.
- The institutional response of the state to deal with the grievances of minorities paved the way for a new political binary: the Hindu majority as a victim of Muslim appeasement versus Muslims as a victim of communalism in the mid-1980s.

Muslims as a defined national minority!

In the post-1992 period, a third feature of being a minority, namely, backwardness and marginalization, evolved. In 1992, the National Commission for Minorities Act was passed, which led to the establishment of the National Commission for Minorities (NCM) in May 1993. The act, in principle, recognized the need to evaluate the reasons behind the relative marginalization of those religious communities which were recognized as minorities at least at the state level.

Following this mandate, the Government of India notified five religious communities: Muslims, Christians, Sikhs, Buddhists and Zoroastrians (Parsis) as national religious minorities in October 1993. This list was amended in 2014, when Jains were notified as a national minority.

Does the act of defining minorities at the national level symbolize a departure from the established constitutional principle? Or is it an extension of the principle—an attempt to fill up the emptiness of the official category called 'minority'?

Indian courts have responded to these questions in an elaborated manner. The judiciary has conceptualized the 'distinctiveness' as the decisive legal criterion. In addition, the courts have also given emphasis to the spatial location of a social group to interpret religious and/or linguistic distinctiveness.

The famous DAV College case of 1971, for instance, very clearly offers us a broad legal principle to recognize a minority. Discussing the interrelationship between Articles 29 and 30 of the Constitution, the Supreme Court conceptualizes 'distinctiveness' as the decisive legal criterion.[8]

The court also discussed the spatial location of a social group to substantiate and concretize its own interpretation of religious and/or linguistic distinctiveness. It is argued:

Though there was a faint attempt to canvas the position that religious or linguistic minorities should be minorities in relation to the entire population of the country, in our view they are to be determined only in relation to the particular legislation which is sought to be impugned, namely that if it is the state legislature, these minorities have to be determined in relation to the population of the state [. . .] It is undisputed, and it was also conceded by the State of Punjab, that the Hindus of Punjab are a religious minority in the state though they may not be so in relation to the entire country.[9]

The observation that a minority should always be recognized at the level of the state has actually evolved into a legal principle in later years. For instance, in the T.M.A. Pai case, the Supreme Court once again asserted, 'With regard to a state law, the unit to determine a religious or linguistic minority can only be the state.'[10]

The notification of a few 'national religious minorities' by the Central government is not seen as a deviation from established legal principles, especially by statutory bodies like the the NCM. In an official note to the ministry of home and the nodal ministry, dated 30 July 1997, the NCM clarifies:

A national-level minority shall have the status of a minority in the entire country irrespective of its local population. This will be so even in a state, region or district where such a minority is factually not a minority in numerical terms. In a particular state, a religious community which is not a national minority recognized by the NCM Act (like the Jews and Bahai) may be recognized as a regional minority.[11]

This note also makes another interesting point to justify the government notification of 1992. Evoking the constitutional commitment to affirmative action, it is argued:

There is thus nothing in the Constitution making it doubtful whether minorities based on religion or language can be lawfully identified as particular classes of citizens requiring special protections and safeguards. On the contrary, all intrinsic aid to the interpretation of the Constitution, as also the up to date judicial trend, point out that religious minorities—like religion-based Scheduled Castes—can be treated as specific identities entitled to special protection by the state.[12]

The relationship between 'distinctiveness' and 'backwardness' as the two determining principles to define a religious group as a constitutional minority, we must note, is not a fully resolved legal issue. There is a strong possibility that distinctiveness might be understood primarily in terms of the numerical inferiority of a community in a particular geo-cultural context; hence, the spatial location of a group becomes a significant point of reference for the judiciary to identify a minority at the state level.

On the other hand, backwardness is a much broader concept, which points towards various national-level processes of social exclusions. In this case, a community of backward communities living in different spatial locations may also be interpreted as a minority, with reference to national population of different social–religious groups.

For example, Muslims in the state of Bihar constitute a distinct religious community; therefore, they are recognized as a state minority. At the same time, Muslims are also recognized as a national minority by the NCM Act, 1992, as their overall 'development' at the national level has been an important policy concern.

In other words, if a minority is to be defined with regard to a national law, the national status of a community has to be taken into consideration; however, if it is a 'state legislature, these minorities have to be determined in relation to the population of the state'. (1971 AIR 1737, 1971 SCR 688).

The contest between 'undefined minority' and 'defined minority' found an interesting manifestation in relation to the recent debate on citizenship. In July 2016, the government introduced the Citizenship Amendment Bill in the Lok Sabha. The bill amends the Citizenship Act, 1955, to make illegal migrants who are Hindus, Sikhs, Buddhists, Jains, Parsis and Christians from Afghanistan, Bangladesh and Pakistan eligible for Indian citizenship. The 'Objective of the Bill' statement states:

> Many persons of Indian origin including persons belonging to . . . minority communities from the aforesaid countries have been applying for citizenship under Section 5 of the Act, but are unable to produce proof of their Indian origin. Hence, they are forced to apply for citizenship by naturalization under Section 6 of the Act, which, inter alia, prescribes twelve years residency as qualification for naturalization in terms of the Third Schedule to the Act. This denies them many opportunities and advantages that may accrue only to the citizens of India, even though they are likely to stay in India permanently. It is proposed to amend the Third Schedule to the Act to make applicants belonging to minority communities from the aforesaid countries eligible for citizenship by naturalization in seven years instead of the existing twelve years.[13]

The bill, as it appears, relies heavily on the defined category of 'religious minority' in only three neighbouring countries (Afghanistan, Bangladesh and Pakistan) where Muslims are in the majority. In this sense, the bill seems to underline the argument that the religious configuration of minority–majority in India is inextricably linked to a few particular countries of South Asia.[14]

Four crucial issues are important to underline here:

- In 1992, a process of defining the minorities on a permanent basis began.
- Only five national religious minorities have been notified by the state. This does not apply to the linguistic minorities.
- A minority can only be identified at the state level for the purpose of constitutionally recognized minority rights. However, for identifying the backwardness and marginalization of a community as a minority, the national status of the minority would be taken into consideration.
- This overlapping and contradiction between the national status of five religious communities as national minorities and the legal principle that a minority shall always be identified at the state level has contributed a lot to the actual politics.

Muslim as a minority and 'Sabka Saath'

We must remember that the NCM Act of 1992 was an outcome of the post–Babri Masjid Congress politics. The move to declare five religious communities as national minorities, in a way, also strengthened the already worked out imagination of 'Hindu majority'. It had now become easier for Hindu essentialists to argue that minorities, especially Muslims, are appeased and pampered at the national level. This argument evolved into political rhetoric in the mid-1990s to underline Hindu subjugation.

The UPA regime initiated some interesting academic politics of minority. Such politics had two very clear facets—it was primarily concerned with appointing various study-based commissions and, at the same time, it aimed at deconstructing the minority category.

The manner in which Muslims are differentiated from other minority religious groups in the post-2000 period, especially after the publication of the *Sachar Committee Report*, is a revealing example of this politics. No doubt that the report was successful in legitimizing Muslim backwardness as a political issue, but this study did not have any direct impact on the actual socio-economic status of Muslims (as revealed by the *Post-Sachar Evaluation Report*, 2014).

Yet, the report emerged as a symbol of Muslim appeasement. The BJP appropriated it to produce a powerful narrative of equality-based affirmative action. The slogan 'Sabka Saath, Sabka Vikas' is often presented as 'development of all and appeasement of none'. In fact, Muslim appeasement has become the dominant narrative in Indian politics. No political group is interested in deviating from this majoritarian impulse in the name of opposing appeasement!

The debate on the minority status of Jamia is a very relevant example. Jamia Millia Islamia (university) was established in 1920 by a section of Muslims as a 'nationalist' educational institution. It became a central university in 1988. The university continued to function as a secular institution; yet, its minority character has always been a contested issue.

The creation of the National Commission for Minority Educational Institutions (NCMEI) in 2004 gave a new twist to Jamia's minority status debate. The UPA 1 government established the NCMEI to respond to the promises it had made in its manifesto. This specific body was formed primarily to protect the rights of minorities to establish and administer the educational institutions of their choice.

The Jamia Teachers Association and the Jamia Old Boys' Association filed petitions in 2006 to NCMEI demanding that at least 50 per cent of students from the Muslim community should be admitted. It was also argued that appropriate action should be taken against the vice chancellor and registrar of the university for the non-implementation of the mandate of the Jamia Millia Islamia Society.

Responding to these arguments, the NCMEI in its judgement says:

> (We) [. . .] have no hesitation in holding that the Jamia was founded by the Muslims for the benefit of Muslims and it never lost its identity as a Muslim minority educational institution, hence, Jamia is a minority educational institution.[15]

The 1988 Jamia Act tells us that Jamia is open to all and it is bound to follow the reservation policy of the government of India. The NCMEI judgement, however, gives a different interpretation. It recognizes Jamia as a Muslim minority institution. Since the 93rd Constitution Amendment Act ensures that minority institutions are exempted from following the national reservation policy, it becomes possible for Jamia to provide reservation to Muslims.

Muslims in the Jamia case are interpreted as national minorities by relying entirely on the principle of cultural distinctiveness. It simply means that the principle of backwardness is not considered applicable to minority-run institutions. In other words, the subgrouping of national minorities—with regard to socio-economic backwardness proposed by the Sachar Committee and the Ranganath Misra Commission—is not taken into consideration.

This poses an apparent contradiction. On the one hand, there is a demand to expand the scope of the SC category so that Muslims and Christians Dalits may get the benefit of reservation. On the other hand, there is no reservation for Muslims Dalits and Christian Dalits in the Muslim and Christian minority-run institutions such as Jamia and St Stephens.[16]

It is apparent that defining a religious minority at the national level is an unsettled issue. The judiciary as well as the Parliament must offer a solution to the tension between the principle of distinctiveness and the principle of backwardness.

The minority status of Muslims of India has now become a highly contested issue—not merely for the Muslims but also for all those who believe in the political morality envisaged by the Constitution of India.

6

Muslims as Backward

'Sir, you did not say anything on it'!

Demand to include Dalit Muslims have been raised for last one and half decades [. . .] the Presidential Order, 1950 eventually confined [sic] SC status to Hindus [. . .] Sir, I request the government to amend the Presidential Order, 1950 so as to add [the] word 'Muslim' in it along with Hindu, Sikh and Buddhist so that the Arzal Muslims who constitute 0.8 per cent of population improve their social, educational and economic status and participate in the process of nation building.[1]

—Ejaz Ali, MP, Rajya Sabha
Proceedings, 2 December 2009)

Husain Dalwai: Sir, I have a question. We have raised the question of Dalit Muslims and Dalit Christians. You did not say anything on it.[2]

Thawar Chand Gehlot (minister for social justice and empowerment): Sir, these two groups do not figure in the list of those social groups which are recognized as Scheduled Caste under the Indian constitutional system. This question is under judicial consideration before the honourable Supreme Court. If a situation emerges after the judicial verdict, this would be taken up for discussion. Otherwise, the government does not approve of it.[3]

—Rajya Sabha debate, 8 December 2014

Muslim backwardness, or exclusion, emerged as one of the most dominant political issues after the publication of the *Sachar Committee Report* in 2006. The findings of the report were used to reiterate the demand for a specific policy package for Muslims. It was stridently argued that addressing Muslims as a backward community (such as the SC, ST, OBC) should not be interpreted as a deviation from constitutional principles and/or secularism.[4]

This enthusiasm for a policy package for Muslims eventually died down after the 2014 elections. In my view, the BJP government refused to acknowledge the backwardness of Muslims as a legitimate policy concern. The impact of this straightforward refusal was so powerful that within a period of three years, all the so-called secular political parties, including the Congress, lost interest in what used to be called the agenda of 'Muslim empowerment'!

Interestingly, public discussions on Muslim empowerment continue to revolve around the resolves and political moves of major political parties. Internal debates among Muslims, especially the imagination of Muslim victimhood envisaged by Muslim elites, have not been systematically analysed so far. This is what this chapter attempts do. It tries to unpack various shades of contemporary Muslim politics of social justice, especially its 'Dalit Muslim' version. The chapter raises two very basic questions:

First, how do Muslim political groups conceptualize the idea of social justice in postcolonial India, especially in the 1990s?

Source: Vikram Nayak.

Second, how do these different notions of social justice deal with the question of Muslim/Islamic homogeneity?

These internal debates, I believe, not only introduce us to the various interpretations of 'Muslim backwardness' but also underline a crucial link between the state's affirmative action and the changing nature of Muslim politics of backwardness.

Dalit Muslims are Indians, and yet Islam is alien!

The legal–constitutional schema that India as a republic adopted after 1950 transformed terms such as 'minority', 'Scheduled Caste', and 'Scheduled Tribe' into secular administrative categories to respond to various forms of sociological and cultural diversity.

For instance, if a social group is culturally/religiously/linguistically distinct and numerically inferior, it might be recognized as a minority; if a social group had experienced caste discrimination and/or untouchability in the past, it would be included in the Scheduled Castes list; and the indigenous communities or tribes are to be officially recognized as Scheduled Tribes. Since minority, SC and ST (and later the Other Backward Classes, the OBC) are conceived as open secular administrative templates, no social group, technically speaking, would become a permanent constituent of these official–secular classifications.

An important question arises here: If the rights of minorities are primarily concerned with the protection of cultural/religious distinctiveness, why do we need to discuss the socio-economic and educational backwardness of members of officially recognized minority groups? This question is important because the Constitution makes provisions to identify the backwardness of social groups and encourages the state to design appropriate policies to tackle this backwardness.

The *Report of the First Backward Classes Commission* is a revealing example of this point. The commission, popularly known as the Kaka Kalelkar Commission, intended to identify the backwardness of the non-SC and non-ST communities. The commission's response to Muslim backwardness, especially in relation to caste-based social stratification among Muslims, is very intriguing. The report notes:

There were representatives on behalf of some Muslim organizations asking that all Muslims should be treated as backward and be given educational aid and adequate representation in government service. It would not be fair, or just, to list all Muslims as socially and educationally backward. *Officially, Muslims do not recognize any caste.* It must be said to the credit of Islam that it did not compromise its position in the matter of untouchables [. . .] gradually, however, Islamic society in India succumbed to the influence of caste and lost its pristine purity. The racial distinction of Mughal and Pathan, Shaikh and Syed has been maintained though, without any sense of social inferiority. We have recognized this deterioration that has overcome Muslim society today and added the names of such backward communities found among them in [the] list of other backward classes.[5]

Despite identifying the internal divisions among Muslims, the report does not give adequate attention to crucial sociological differences in the wider context of affirmative action. It lists the relative marginalization of those who are socially/culturally treated as inferior in a somehow mechanical manner, simply abiding by the Nehruvian policy of non-interference in the affairs of minorities.

The Presidential Order, 1950 (that has been amended twice), is another relevant example, which actually restricts the entry of Muslim and Christian castes into the SC list. The order says:

The castes, races or tribes or parts of, or groups within, castes or tribes [. . .] shall, in relation to the States to which those Parts respectively related, be deemed to be Scheduled Castes.

However, this general definition of Scheduled Castes is further clarified. The next paragraph of the order notes:

No person who professes a religion different from the Hindu, the Sikh or the Buddhist religion shall be deemed to be a member of a Scheduled Caste.[6]

Here it is clear that in order to avail of the benefit of SC reservation, the members of the identified scheduled castes would have to stay within the Hindu fold. Socially backward Muslims and Christians are not entitled to SC reservation. This does not apply to the ST and OBC categories though. Muslim and Christian communities can be included in the ST and OBC lists. In other words, conversion to Christianity and Islam by the weaker sections is officially identified as a serious challenge to the very nature of affirmative-action policies.

The view that the purpose of reservation is to reform and protect the integrity of Hindu society seems to prevail in recent years. The Dissent Note of the member secretary of the Misra Commission is a good example. This note argues:

The positive discrimination on the ground of social and economic backwardness arising out of untouchability was granted to certain castes professing Hinduism with the objective of achieving the constitutional guarantee of equality [. . .] *Both Islam and Christianity are religions, which originated outside India.* These came from foreign lands to India along with traders, invaders and preachers/missionaries over a period of time spanning hundreds of years and firmly established themselves as more and more indigenous people converted from their religion to Islam/Christianity. Both are religions that do not recognize caste. It may be extremely difficult to hazard a guess about the number of the progeny of such traders/invaders/preachers/settlers from foreign lands and Scheduled Castes who converted the present population of Muslims/Christians in India. What can, however, be said with an element of certainty is that a vast majority of Muslims and Christians in India today comprise the converts and their progeny.[7]

This observation very clearly establishes that the purpose of reservation in India is simply to reform Hinduism. It is asserted that those communities which had opted out of the original Hindu religion in the past are not entitled to positive discrimination simply because of two reasons:

(a) Embracing Islam or Christianity means accepting a faith that is intrinsically alien to the caste-based Indian social order.
(b) Leaving Hinduism means the end of exploitation based on untouchability.

In this sense, the freedom of religion, both in terms of 'propagation of religion' as well as accepting other religions is understood with reference to an unstated order of religions. The religions of Indian origin—Hinduism, Sikhism, Buddhism and Jainism—constitute the core of Indian religiosity in this schema, while Islam and Christianity are seen as floating external ideas.

Yes, Muslims are backward! Two perspectives, four positions

Let us look at Muslim intellectual political responses to the question of Muslim backwardness. For the sake of clarity, I discuss two broad perspectives on Muslim reservation. The first perspective, which I call the 'Muslim unity perspective', argues that Muslims as a whole are backward and marginalized. Therefore, it is important to develop a kind of social justice regime that could address the problems and issues of all Muslims in India. The internal caste/class differences, it is claimed, need to be solved internally, at the community level, through negotiations, so that the collective strength of all Indian Muslims could be used to bargain with the state.

The second perspective, which could be called the Muslim Pasmand perspective, highlights the internal divisions, especially the caste differences, among Muslims. It shows that Muslims, like Hindus, are divided on caste lines. The upper caste, which is also an upper class, uses the social hierarchy to subjugate backward/lower-caste Muslims. Thus, the empowerment of marginalized Muslims should be taken up as the most important agenda, not only for the internal democratization of the Muslim community but also to achieve real and legitimate social justice in India.

For the purpose of discussion, I examine the ideas and politics of four leading Muslim political intellectuals of north India. The choice of these political elites is not entirely arbitrary. Factors such as political experience, caste background, educational training, professional career and, above all, their public presence as Muslim figures have been taken into consideration.

Instead of describing who does what, let us talk about the following four questions, which simply try to find logical coherence in the ideas of these political ideologues, especially in relation to social injustice and social justice.

1. What is 'injustice'?
2. What are the sources of this injustice?
3. What is to be done to deal with this injustice?
4. What are the justifications? What is the scope of social justice?

'Universalize reservation for Muslims!'

The late Syed Shahabuddin, who was Syed by caste (an Ashraf caste), had a brilliant career as a civil servant before joining active politics in 1977. He was an ex-MP. Shahabuddin established the first Muslim political coalition on the question of the Babri Masjid in 1987.

What is 'injustice'? What are the sources of this injustice?
For Shahabuddin, the centralization of power is the most important problem in the Indian system. Because of this centralization, established institutions are not performing the functions they are expected to. Shahabuddin identifies two aspects of this centralization. First, there is a lack of adequate representation of different groups in the institutions and, therefore, power gets centralized. Secondly, the dominant group is not only using the state apparatus for its own vested interests but also trying to demolish the fundamental structure of the Indian state—the Nehru–Gandhi model—thus, there is a perpetuation of the process of centralization. He writes:

> In India we are reaching the intersection, the point of explosion. The tribal unrest, the militancy among the dalits, the upsurge among the OBCs, and the dissatisfaction among the minorities are no more than signals [. . .] They (dominant group) promise all that [sic] everything except land to tiller, living wages to workers, proportional reservation of public employment, universal and compulsory education.[8]

What is to be done to deal with this injustice?
Shahabuddin thinks that reservation for all Muslims could be a possible way out. However, we find two very different positions taken by him on this question. Initially, he argued that in the case of Indian Muslims, caste identity could not be separated from

religious identity. He noted that the reservation for backward Muslims was, sociologically, a valid demand. However, this demand should be seen in relation to the wider Muslim demand for OBC status. Therefore, he opposed the SC status for Muslim Dalits in 2004.[9]

But, later, his position changed. In his introductory speech at the Muslim Convention for Reservation in 2009, he accepted the Dalit Muslim demand for reservation. He said:

> The Muslim community should have a separate sub-quota as a backward class, in proportion to its national/state population and its relative backwardness, as determined on the basis of uniform prescribed parameter [. . .] The Muslim sub-communities, which are on par with SCs and which have [in] some state[s] been included in the OBC lists, should be admitted to the SC list and the religious bar in the Constitutional (SC) Order, 1950, issued under Article 341 of the Constitution should be included and Para 3 of the Order should be deleted. In order to fulfil the sub-quota of 10–15 per cent for the minorities and meet the demands of other groups, [the] Central government must move [the] SC to remove the bar of 50 per cent on total reservation, if necessary by legislation, because a uniform bar for the entire country which has varying number of backward classes with varying levels of backwardness in different states is neither rational nor necessary.[10]

What are the justifications? What is the scope of social justice?
Shahabuddin gives two justifications: one is legal while the other is theoretical. According to him, Article 16 (4) of the Constitution, which says: 'Nothing in this article shall prevent the State from making any provision for the reservation of appointments or posts in favour of any backward class of citizens which, in the opinion of the State, is not adequately represented in the services under the State,' could also be read differently. He argues that Muslims could be recognized as a

backward class under the purview of Article 16 (4) of the Constitution because this article does not specifically mention that a religious community cannot be recognized as a backward class.

In order to understand this reading of the Constitution, let us look at his theoretical justification. He proposes a theory of 'universal reservation'. According to him, 'I would have no problem with a modified reservation system which breaks up the artificial conglomerates of SCs, STs OBCs and minorities and introduces a regime of *universal reservation with separate quotas for every identifiable and self-conscious subgroup (religious, caste, racial, geographic, linguistic and cultural) in proportion to its population and its index of backwardness at every operational level.* Even if, in the event of a Muslim quota under the present system, any Muslim subgroup which comprises more than 1 per cent of the total population wishes to have its own sub-quota, I have no objection, though it may weaken the bargaining capacity of the community in other respects.'[11]

So, for Shahabuddin, social justice is:

1. All Muslims should be given reservation under the OBC category because they are backward and more so because the fruits of reservation need to be distributed among all groups.
2. There should be a creamy-layer provision, based on the socio-economic conditions of Muslims.
3. Muslim Dalits should be included in the SC list.
4. There should be a sub-quota for Muslim subcommunities in the proposed Muslim quota.
5. Reservation should also be given in the private sectors.

'Quota/Sub-quota!'

The late Iqbal Ansari was Ansari by caste (an Ashraf caste). He was a retired professor of English at Aligarh Muslim University.

He is the author of two seminal works—one on minorities and the other on Muslim political representation. Ansari was also an active human rights activist.

What is 'injustice'? What are the sources of this injustice?
Ansari's work is based on two assumptions:

(a) There are some collective identifiable interests of a pan-Indian Muslim community.
(b) Reservation is an essential means to safeguard these collective interests in the existing legal–constitutional framework.[12]

Ansari focuses on the question of under-representation. For him, Muslims as an identifiable social category are under-represented in all spheres, including services and legislative bodies in postcolonial India. This unjust representation is the root cause of all problems. Ansari's position on the Mandal Commission's recommendations, especially with regard to non-Hindu OBCs, may be taken as an example to elaborate this point.

According to him:

The Mandal Commission's mandate—qualitative and quantitative—based not on empirical study of Muslim social reality but deductionist logic, which made it fix [it at a] grossly low level, i.e., 52 per cent of backwardness among Muslims [. . .] it never occurred to [the] Mandal Commission to go into the issue of discrimination, neglect and intolerance that Muslims routinely faced because of the strong sub-group loyalty of all Hindus and because of 'otherness' imposed upon Muslims, especially in the Hindi belt and Gujarat. If the commission's concern for social justice had been extended to Muslims, it should have recommended a separate quota for at least those Muslim groups whom it had identified as OBCs. Why did

Mandal's concern for justice not make him recommend a separate quota for backward Muslims?[13]

What is to be done to deal with this injustice?
Ansari gives three very clear-cut legal–constitutional answers.

1. Following Shahabuddin, he too asserts that Article 16(4) can also be read to include all Muslims in the OBC lists as a backward class. In addition, he goes one step further and suggests that the word 'minorities' should be included in the text of Articles 15(4) and 16 (4).

2. Ansari suggests that all Muslims should be included in the OBC lists. However, a sub-quota within this category could be reserved for those castes which are traditionally 'backward'. He also suggests that a new method of determining the creamy layer should be worked out. In case of the non-availability of suitable candidates from these 'backward' castes, the remaining share in the sub-quota could be made available to the general Muslims.

3. If the entire Muslim community is not provided reservation, there should be a fixed quota in the existing OBC quota for OBC Muslims. Ansari says: 'I hold the opinion that in any formulation on reservation for Muslims, the creamy layer, defined in terms of education, income and occupation, must be excluded irrespective of racial or country origin over a millennium, and that backwardness needs to be redefined taking into account socio-economic changes among Muslims.'[14]

What are the justifications? What is the scope of social justice?
Ansari justifies his vision of social justice on two counts.

1. There are some very specific Muslims problems, such as wider discrimination and a sense of insecurity, which need to be

recognized with regard to Muslim marginalization. Therefore, the demand for declaring the Muslim community as a backward class is legally as well as constitutionally justifiable. (Ansari, 2004)

2. The Indian State must also recognize recent international forms of affirmative action, especially UN initiatives related to minority rights. So the demand for reservation is also justified on the basis of international discourse on human rights.[15]

Thus, for Ansari, social justice is:

1. Muslim reservation as an expansion of minority right.
2. Muslim reservation, as an idea, has historical roots because it was very much included in the first draft of the Constitution.
3. Internal contradictions among Muslims should be resolved by adopting more advanced legal mechanisms, such as a sub-quota within the larger Muslim quota or a quota for Muslim OBCs in the existing OBC quota.

Muslim Pasmanda versus Muslim Ashrafs

Ali Anwar is an ex-MP. He used to be the spokesperson of JD(U). Anwar is Ansari by caste (Arzal caste). He was a trained Hindi journalist before joining politics. He used to be a leftist and has worked with the Communist Party of India in Bihar. His book *Maswat ki Jung* (*Battle for Equality*) is considered to be a path-breaking study on Pasmanda Muslim politics. Ali Anwar is the founder leader of Pasmanda Muslim Mahaz.

What is injustice? What are the sources of this injustice?
According to Anwar, Muslim lower castes, or what he calls Dalits—namely the Ajlaf and Arzal—are the victims of four kinds of unjust systems.

1. They have been socially excluded.
2. They are economically backward.
3. They are not getting the benefit of affirmative action.
4. Because of their Islamic identity, they also face communal discrimination.

Apart from these factors, Anwar also points out that Muslim society in general faces some problems which are very specific to them.[16]

Anwar identifies various reasons behind this injustice. These reasons could be divided into three categories:

1. Historical: He argues that the Muslim caste structure, which was under the direct influence of Hinduism, produced a similar kind of caste hierarchy. As a result, Muslim society is divided on caste lines—Ashraf, Ajlaf and Arzal. 'This social categorization based on social prestige actually established a kind of unjust Muslim social order. It was ironic because Islamic principles do not approve of such social divisions. The majority of the people who got converted to Islam were lower-caste Hindus who found a new hope in the religion. But the caste system did not allow them that space even in the Islamic fold.'[17]
2. Political: Elaborating this problem, Anwar argues that the Ashraf Muslim leadership did not bother to raise the issues of Muslim Dalits. As a result, Muslim Dalits could not be included in the SC list.
3. Social: The Mandal Commission for the first time recognized the position of lower-caste Muslims and recommended that they should be included in the OBC category. The Ashraf leadership, however, has been trying to capture the benefits of the Mandal Commission by demanding that all Muslims be recognized as OBC.[18]

What is needed to deal with this injustice?
Ali Anwar, like Shahabuddin and Ansari, proposes four legal–constitutional solutions, which, in his opinion, are secular in nature:

1. (a) The state should continue to follow a secular policy of affirmative action. All Muslims should not be recognized as OBC because such a move would reproduce the existing social hierarchies among Muslims; (b) The 50 per cent ceiling on reservation imposed by the Supreme Court should be repealed, if the government wants to give reservation to an economically backward class; and (c) The state should also develop policies to help Ashraf Muslims.[19]
2. Muslim Dalits should be included in the SC list. Article 341 should be amended and the SC quota should be increased.
3. The existing Mandal regime is very significant for backward Muslims because it is not based on any communal categorization. However, before taking any position on the existing Mandal framework, we need to conduct a proper survey to determine the actual share of Muslim OBCs.
4. Instead of a separate OBC Muslim quota under the Mandal dispensation, OBCs should be divided into two: (a) Most backward classes and (b) Other OBCs. Both categories would have Hindu and Muslim castes as well as people from other religions, depending on their socio-economic backwardness.

What are the justifications? What is the scope of social justice?
Ali Anwar gives three justifications for his proposals:

1. Constitutional justification: The inclusion of Muslim and Christian Dalits in the SC list is justifiable because the

Sikhs and the neo-Buddhists were given SC status after the infamous Presidential Order of 1950. So if the state recognizes the Dalit Muslims' plea, it will defiantly widen the scope of affirmative action and social justice will be achieved.

2. Political justification: The inclusion of Muslim Dalits into the SC list will strengthen Dalit unity, which is secular in nature. In addition, OBC Muslims under the existing Mandal scheme enjoy the benefit of reservation on the basis of their socio-economic status, which is a non-communal scheme. This is justifiable on the basis of Indian secularism.

Elaborating on his notion of secularism, Anwar says:

The Dalit and backward-caste Muslims are all of indigenous origin, being descendants of converts from the oppressed castes. This is why we don't use the words 'Dalit minority' or 'Dalit Muslim minority' or 'backward caste Muslim minority'. We Dalits and backward castes are not a minority at all. In fact, taken together, we are in the majority, the 'Bahujan', forming over 85 per cent of the Indian population, despite the fact that we might follow different religions. We see that the politics of communalism, fuelled by both Hindu and Muslim elites, is aimed at dividing us, making us fight among ourselves, so that the elites continue to rule over us as they have been doing for centuries. This is why we in the Mahaz have been seeking to steer our people from emotional politics to politics centred on issues of survival and daily existence and social justice, and for this we have been working with non-Muslim Dalit and backward caste movements and groups to struggle jointly for our rights and to oppose the politics of communalism fuelled by Hindu and Muslim 'upper' caste elites.[20]

3. The state should also recognize the common problem of all Muslims, such as communalism, and should protect the minority rights given in the Constitution. He also argues that there should be some general schemes available to deal with the issues of poor Muslim Ashrafs.

This discussion leads us to three aspects of Ali Anwar's notion of social justice:

1. Internal contradictions among the Muslims need to be taken seriously so as to reach out to the truly marginalized Muslims.
2. Affirmative action should be based on secular principles.
3. The state has to play a more important role in dealing with social issues.

'We are opposed to reservations for Muslims as a whole!'

Dr Ejaz Ali (MD) is an ex-MP, Rajya Sabha, from Bihar. He is a Rayeen by caste (Arzal caste). He is a trained surgeon. Ali comes from a political family. His father-in-law was a famous Muslim leader of Bihar—Ghulam Sarwar. Ejaz Ali was one of the very first Dalit Muslim leaders who raised the question of Muslim Dalits in post-1992 Bihar. He has established the All India Backward Muslim Morcha in 1994. In fact, he coined the term 'Dalit Muslims' to describe backward-caste Muslims.

What is injustice? What are the sources of this injustice?
Ejaz Ali, like Ali Anwar, feels that the caste structure is the main problem. He also shares the view that Islamic principles do not recognize caste-like structures, but the Ashraf hegemony, which he calls 'Syedism', established a social order based on caste hierarchies. He says: 'Almost all Muslims in India are descendants of local

converts. Our ancestors did not come from Arabia. They were locals who converted to Islam: the Dalits who converted to Islam en masse, to escape from caste oppression under the Brahminical order.'[21]

So this unjust system of caste led to wider legal–constitutional injustice, which Ali believes is one of the main problems faced by present-day Dalit Muslims. Ali notes:

As the law stands today, Dalit Muslims are denied reservation rights as Scheduled Castes although their conditions are the same as the Hindu Dalits. However, in 1950, a Presidential Order was passed according to which these special benefits would be available only to those Scheduled Castes who professed to be Hindu, and, accordingly, an amendment was made to Article 341 of the Constitution of India that authorizes the President to declare certain castes as Scheduled Castes for special benefits [. . .] We are struggling to have the Presidential Order rescinded so that all Dalits, irrespective of religion, enjoy the same benefits. In 1956, Article 341 was amended to extend the same benefits that Hindu Dalits enjoy to Sikh Dalits, and in 1990, this was extended to the neo-Buddhists. If these communities can enjoy Scheduled Caste status despite belonging to theoretically egalitarian religions, then why not Dalit Muslims and Dalit Christians?[22]

What is needed to deal with this injustice?
Ali classifies Ashrafs, Dalit Muslims and OBC Muslims in different categories. He demands that Dalit Muslims, being the most disadvantaged lot, be given more preferences.

Two solutions can be identified in his writings:

1. Muslim Dalits should be kept out of the OBC list and placed in the SC list. He argues:

Under Mandal, two categories of Muslims have been included as OBCs. The first are the Dalit Muslims, descendants of 'untouchable' converts to Islam. The other category, which is far smaller in number, consists of the Muslim counterparts of social groups among Hindus recognized as OBCs, such as vegetable growers, milkmen, and so on. We would like the former category to be recognized as Scheduled Castes instead of OBCs, as is the case at present. There are two reasons for this. Firstly, because presently, the OBCs are given only benefits of reservations in government jobs and some limited concessions in the matter of education. On the other hand, the Scheduled Castes are provided not just job reservations, but also political reservations in state legislatures and the Parliament, and facilities such as housing schemes, interest-free loans, special courts to try cases of atrocities against them, and so on. As a result of these benefits, the Hindu Dalits have been able to make considerable headway, leaving the Dalit Muslims lagging far behind them. Is it not right that the Dalit Muslims too should be granted similar benefits so that they can also progress? Further, by placing the Dalit Muslims in the same category as economically, socially and educationally far more powerful and advanced Hindu and Muslim OBCs, they have been put at a considerable disadvantage. How can you expect the extremely poor Dalit Muslims to compete with these groups for the limited benefits that are provided for the OBCs? Little wonder then that it is these powerful groups who are cornering all the advantages from the limited implementation of the recommendations of the Mandal Commission Report, while the Dalit Muslims have gained almost nothing from it.[23]

2. All Muslims should not be included in the OBC list. He says:

We are opposed to reservations for Muslims as a whole. The Indian Constitution itself prohibits reservations on a communal basis, for an entire community, and provides for reservations only for socially and educationally backward sections of religious communities. Furthermore, demands for reservations for Muslims as a whole will only further strengthen inter-communal antagonism, and even if introduced, the benefits would accrue to economically and educationally better-off Muslims, not the Dalit Muslims, who form the vast majority of the Muslim population and who need such benefits the most.[24]

What are the justifications? What is the scope of social justice?
Ali gives two justifications for his understanding of reservation:

1. Sociological and political justification: Muslims Dalits are the descendants of those Dalit Hindus who embraced Islam. These Muslim Dalits are still involved in caste-based professions which are considered to be socially inferior. Reservation, if they are included in the SC list, will not only help them in protecting their socio-economic rights but will also provide them an opportunity to elect their political representatives.
2. Religious justification: The empowerment of Dalit Muslims will help in democratizing the internal structure of the Muslim community and establish the real and egalitarian principles of Islam.

So what is social justice from his point of view? We can identify four very interesting points:

1. Muslim caste dynamics are very crucial for making sense of the powerlessness of the Muslim community in India.

2. There is a difference in the problems of Muslim Dalits and Muslim OBCs, and that's why we need a package of affirmative action to deal with the general as well as specific problems of backward Muslims.
3. Political power is also very important; for that reason, Muslim Dalits should be included in the SC list.
4. Muslim unity is important, but to achieve that unity in a true sense the Muslim caste system should end. Islamic principles are egalitarian and there is no place for such social categorization in Islam.

'Dalit Muslims' and the two norms of Muslim politics

The term 'Dalit Muslim' has emerged as one of the most contested categories in recent years. We find that political elites like Shahabuddin and Iqbal Ansari did not initially use the term. Instead, they employed legal concepts such as 'Muslim OBCs' and/or 'Muslim subcommunities' in order to avoid direct discussion on the subject of internal differentiations among Muslims.

The Muslim Pasmanda perspective, however, deliberately emphasized upon the term 'Dalit Muslim' to underline a kind of political assertion against the caste dominance of upper-caste Ashrafs. Ejaz Ali, who coined this term, forcefully argues that Dalit Muslims symbolize the inferior, backward and/or subjugated positions of a number of Muslim castes, known as Arzal *biradari*s. Similarly, Ali Anwar has also tried to expand the scope of the concept of Dalit Muslims by introducing another powerful term, 'Muslim Pasmanda' (Backward). In his opinion, the term 'Pasmanda' reflects the collective assertion of Dalit and backward-caste Muslim organizations.

These apparent contradictions, however, do not prevent the Muslim elites from evolving political consensus on a case-by-case basis. In fact, the conflicts of ideas and positions as well as political agreements and issue-based consensus set the terms of Muslim political discourse, which is often not taken into consideration. Therefore, two aspects of this Muslim-backwardness discourse need to be underlined.

First, the Muslim politics of social justice, especially its Pasmanda perspective, does not entirely go beyond the given notion of Muslim/Islamic homogeneity in India. Despite being critical of Ashraf hegemony, the Pasmanda movements evoke the concept of Dalit Muslim to underline a tension between the exploitative nature of Muslim caste *practice* and egalitarian Islamic *principles*. This adherence to Islamic identity helps them establish effective channels of communication with other Muslim groups.

The Declaration of the Joint Committee for Empowerment, 2009, is a good example in this regard. It argued for the reservation of all Muslims as well as the inclusion of Dalit Muslims in the SC list. The declaration demands:

> The formal recognition of the Muslim community as a backward class in the light of the findings and recommendations of the Sachar Committee and the Misra Commission [. . .] the immediate publication of the Misra Commission Report, full implementation of its basic recommendations [. . .] and the deletion of Para 3 of the Constitution SC order 1950, issued under Article 341 of the Constitution for the inclusion of Muslim and Dalit Christians in the SC list.[25]

This led to the second point. We find that there is a crucial link between the Muslim politics of social justice and the legal–constitutional discourse. All Muslim groups seem to place their political agendas in the grand framework of minority rights and affirmative action. This explicit faithfulness to legal constitutionalism appears to function as a norm of Muslim politics.

It would be interesting to observe the functioning of these norms of Muslim politics in the wake of radical Hindutva. This is what we discuss in the last few chapters of this book.

Source: Vikram Nayak.

7

The Politics of Triple Talaq

Triple talaq as an MCQ!

The question of 'triple talaq' is posed as an objective-type MCQ (multiple choice question)! We are given two options—support it (say yes) or oppose it (say no). The meaning of yes and no are also premeditated in this schema: Yes refers to closed Islamism, while No stands for gender equality and progress.

This dominant (and somewhat stereotypical) representation of the triple talaq issue is based on a few strong assumptions about Muslims in general and Muslim men in particular:

- The Muslims of India constitute a single, closed, homogeneous community, which is inevitably male-dominated.
- This male-dominated community is governed by a few established Islamic norms which are highly anti-women in nature. Islamic religiosity as well as Islamic practices, hence, are intrinsically patriarchal.
- The Islamic clergy functions as the true representative of the community. It has an ultimate right to interpret religious texts and, at the same time, speak on behalf of all Muslims.

These convictions, interestingly, are often presented to us as hard facts—not merely by the government, political parties and the ulema class but also by those who prefer to be identified as 'liberals'. As a result, a media-centric discourse of political correctness emerges, which virtually freezes any possibility of a nuanced and meaningful discussion on the nature and functions of patriarchy among Muslims.

The recent debate on triple talaq is an example of such stereotypical public imagination. No one bothered to look at the arguments and positions of various Muslim women's groups on the status of Muslim women in India, the internal debates among them on the question of Muslim patriarchy, their varied interpretations of the Quran and Hadith, their critical responses to the much-debated idea of the Uniform Civil Code and, above all, their critique of Muslim personal law and the role of the ulema in nurturing the anti-Muslim attitude of Hindutva politics.

The triple talaq debate, surprisingly, is seen as a battle between the conservative ulema represented by the All Indian Muslim Personal Law Board (AIMPLB) and the committed BJP-led NDA government. The discussion in the Parliament on the triple talaq bill and, later, on the triple talaq ordinance seems to ignore the nuanced arguments made by Muslim women's groups, especially the Bharatiya Muslim Mahila Andolan (BMMA). The purpose, therefore, of this chapter is to clarify and contextualize the public debate so as to make sense of the various aspects of the controversy. In addition, an attempt is made to analyse the politics of triple talaq in the wake of emerging Hindutva.

Let us begin with a few frequently used terms:

- 'Triple talaq' refers to a practice which empowers a man to divorce his wife by saying 'talaq, talaq, talaq' in one go.
- 'Mehr' is a sum of money or other property to be delivered to the bride by the bridegroom at the time of the nikah as

a prerequisite for the solemnization of their marriage, as specified in the *nikahnama*.

- 'Iddat' is the period of time (approximately three to four months) during which a divorced woman/widow cannot remarry another man.
- 'Nikah' is a contract of marriage between a man and a woman. The nikahnama is a document which specifies the terms and conditions of this agreement.
- 'Sharia' or 'shariat' is a collection of rules and norms that have been codified following the Quran and Hadith (laying out the sayings and acts of Prophet Muhammad). Since this codification is subject to various interpretations, there are various shariats among Sunnis and Shias.
- *'Nikah halala'* is also a frequently used term. Once a woman has been divorced, her husband is not permitted take her back as his wife unless the woman undergoes nikah halala, which involves her marriage with another man who subsequently divorces her so that her previous husband can remarry her.

The practice of triple talaq, we must note, is legitimate among Sunni Muslims of the Hanafi shariat. Although we do not have adequate statistical information about the sect-wise population of Muslims in India, it is believed that Sunni Hanafis are in the majority, at least in the northern states. But there are four other schools of Sunni shariat—Hanbali, Shafi, Maliki and Ahle-Hadith. These schools have their own interpretations of rituals and customs and specific norms for divorce. The AIMPLB itself recognizes this Islamic religious plurality in India. In fact, one of the stated objectives of the AIMPLB is:

To promote goodwill, fraternity and the feeling of mutual cooperation among all sects and schools of thought among Muslims, and to generate the spirit of unity and coordination

among them for the common goal of safeguarding the Muslim
Personal Law.[1]

There are two questions are important here: Does the AIMPLB
determine the everyday conduct of the religiously diversified
Muslim communities? If so, do Muslims, particularly the followers
of the Hanafi shariat, practise triple talaq precisely because of their
religious adherence to Islam?

Muslim contestation over triple talaq

The survey conducted by the BMMA is very relevant in this
regard. The report, entitled 'No More Talaq Talaq Talaq:
Muslim Women Call for Ban on an Un-Islamic Practice', which
is based on an extensive survey, argues that over 92 per cent
of Muslim women in India are not in favour of the practice
of verbal triple talaq. The report also discusses 117 specific
cases where triple talaq was practised and women were divorced
without their consent.[2]

A close reading of these testimonies suggests that triple talaq
is actually used by Muslim men as a legitimate religious weapon
to subjugate women. The report finds dowry demands, not giving
birth to a male child and the husband's affair with another woman
to be some of the main reasons for divorce. The report claims
that these sociocultural issues produce and sustain various forms
of patriarchal power structures.

In order to justify this specific Indo-Muslim form
of patriarchy, the report argues, a selective anti-women
interpretation of the Quran is employed. This is the reason why
many women are deprived of the legitimate mehr amount after
the divorce, which is supposed to be given to them at the time
of marriage. Evoking the centrality of the gender question, the
report stridently contends:

Muslim orthodoxy in India does not want to entertain any talk of personal law reform and the Hindu right is pushing for the Uniform Civil Code (UCC). The truth is both these sections are coming from extreme points-of-view and both are equally patriarchal.[3]

A powerful argument in favour of Islamic reform is also asserted:

We have to begin a process of [. . .] social reform involving the whole community and the elected representatives. Indian democracy allows for regulation of family matters based on each one's religious texts. The Christian and the Parsi minorities have taken recourse to these Constitutional provisions and enacted their personal laws accordingly. It is the Muslim orthodoxy signified in the self-appointed personal law body that is resistant to any reform within the agreed framework. It is anybody's guess as to how representative this body is as far as the Indian Muslim population is concerned.[4]

The writ petition filed by the Shayara Bano in the Supreme Court also makes a similar argument. (Though, unlike the BMMA, it favours the UCC). There are five main demands made by Shayara Bano in this case:

• The divorce deed issued by her husband should be treated as illegal and unconstitutional as it violates Articles 14, 15, 21 and 25 of the Constitution.
• Section 2 of the Muslim Personal Law (Shariat) Application Act, 1937, should be declared unconstitutional as it seeks to recognize and validate *talaq-e-bidat* (triple talaq) as a valid form of divorce, the practice of nikah halala and the practice of polygamy.
• The Dissolution of Muslim Marriages Act, 1939, should be declared unconstitutional as it fails to secure for Indian Muslim women protection from bigamy.

- The practice of polygamy should be declared illegal and unconstitutional.
- A Muslim woman whose marriage has been terminated by a valid and legally recognized form of talaq by her husband may remarry her husband without an intervening halala marriage with another man.[5]

These five demands should also be read in relation to the ongoing debate on the UCC. The petition calls upon the state to implement the UCC (which is, in any case, simply a proposal!) to secure and protect the constitutional rights of Muslim women. But at the same time, gender-sensitive interpretations of Islamic texts are also evoked to condemn the practice of triple talaq as an un-Islamic, inhuman and unconstitutional custom. In other words, Shayara Bano's petition does not find any conflict between the gender-just UCC and the Islamic religious identity of Muslim women.

Since Shayara Bano does not give up her Islamic identity and even goes on to challenge the claim made by the AIMPLB as the sole custodian of Islam, the AIMPLB finds it difficult to take a conventional 'Islam in danger' type position this time. The AIMPLB's counter affidavit actually underlines an interesting unease. It opposes the writ petition on five grounds. It states:

- The questions raised in the petition are matters of legislative policy.
- Personal laws cannot be challenged as being violative of Part III of the Constitution.
- The personal laws of a community cannot be rewritten in the name of social reform.
- Article 44 of the Constitution of India, which envisages a Uniform Civil Code, is only a directive principle of state policy and is not enforceable.

- Muslim personal law is based on holy scriptures—Al-Quran and sources based on the same.[6]

The last two justifications are important. The AIMPLB poses the issue of the UCC as legally problematic and religiously unacceptable. If the AIMPLB believes that Islamic shariat (or shariats) constitutes a 'complete way of life', why is there is no demand to implement shariat laws in relation to those 'criminal cases' in which Muslims are involved?

The affidavit also uses Islam selectively to counter Shayara Bano's petition. It says:

Almost 90 per cent of Indian Muslims are Sunni Hanafi, and the rest 10 per cent consist of Shafais and Ahle-Hadiths. Shafais endorse the Hanafi stance on this issue that triple talaq in one go constitutes effective talaq and results in the immediate termination of marriage.[7]

But what about Ahle-Hadiths who do not subscribe to this practice of triple talaq?

It is worth mentioning that the general secretary of the Ahle Hadith, Maulana Asghar Ali Imam Mehdi, in an interview, said:

We oppose the idea of triple talaq. This is not in keeping with the Quran and Hadith. We treat talaq said thrice in one go as one utterance only and taking full cognizance of how the Quran frowns upon divorce and advocates measured and patient attempts at reconciliation and the presence of proper 'panches' or wise counsel-givers in the process, we are opposed to this form of talaq.[8]

The AIMPLB's counter affidavit does not pay attention to this form of Islam. It goes on to defend not merely triple talaq but also the practice of nikah halala, polygamy and, above all, the superiority of men over women!

Let us sum up this highly diversified internal Muslim debate on triple talaq:

- The conventional ulema representing the AIMPLB support the practice of triple talaq on legal as well as religious grounds.
- The Ahle-Hadith sect of Sunnis opposes the practice of triple talaq on religious grounds without challenging the AIMPLB directly.
- The BMMA opposes triple talaq on religious, social and cultural grounds, but it is not in favour of the UCC.
- The writ petition filed by Shayara Bano and others opposes triple talaq on constitutional and Islamic grounds. However, they argue for a gender-sensitive UCC.

Supreme Court judgement

In August 2017, the Supreme Court delivered its much-awaited judgement on the triple talaq case. Notwithstanding the media hype, this nuanced judgement was not adequately discussed. As a result, public discussions continued to revolve around the claims and counterclaims made by the two dominant stakeholders—the AIMPLB and the overenthusiastic government. Interestingly, both of them celebrated the judgement and described it legally appropriate and socially egalitarian! Muslim women's groups and women petitioners were seen as voiceless sufferers whose cause is represented by the government. The question is: If it was a win-win situation for all, who was the loser in this case?

The Supreme Court systematically explored the issue of triple talaq and tried to locate it in the realm of constitutional law. Written in a highly lucid and argumentative manner, the verdict made it clear that the judicial proceedings should be separated from media-driven political discussions. This clarity is invoked to argue that the triple talaq phenomenon is inextricable linked to the legislative competence of the Parliament and the task of the judiciary is simply to explicate the nuances involved in this unjust practice.

There are three arguments inherent in the judgement. First, the court does not find any reason to interpret triple talaq or 'talaq-e-biddat' as a violation of Article 25. It is emphasized that this practice does not go against the other fundamental rights given to citizens, such as equality before law and the prohibition of discrimination on the grounds of religion, race, caste, etc. In fact, the court identified this practice as an inseparable constituent of Muslim personal law. (However, it also makes it very clear that personal law in the context of triple talaq only refers to the shariat governing the Hanafi School of Sunni Islam.) It is argued:

> We have arrived at the conclusion, that 'talaq-e-biddat', is a matter of 'personal law' of Sunni Muslims, belonging to the Hanafi School. It constitutes a matter of their faith. It has been practised by them, for at least 1400 years. We have examined whether the practice satisfies the constraints provided for under Article 25 of the Constitution, and have arrived at the conclusion, that it does not breach any of them. We have also come to the conclusion, that the practice being a component of 'personal law' has the protection of Article 25 of the Constitution.[9]

The second argument goes beyond these legal technicalities and addresses the most contentious issue: the reforms in Muslim personal law. Recognizing the fact that triple talaq is a social–religious problem, the judgement unequivocally argues that this evil practice must be banned, for creating a gender-just and egalitarian social order.

At the same time, however, the court clarifies that the task of the judiciary is to evaluate the merits and demerits of a social question from the point of view of constitutional law. This statutory power does not authorize the court to intervene in the legislative sphere of the Parliament. Likewise, the judiciary cannot get involved in the religious sphere of the communities either. If a religious practice becomes socially complicated, the Parliament—being the representative body—should come forward and initiate the process of reforms, including in the realm of personal laws.

This reasoning is justified on historical grounds. The court argues that the reforms to personal law in India, with regard to socially and culturally unacceptable practices in different religions, have transpired only by way of legislative intervention. The Constitution empowers the Parliament to make adequate laws to reform religious practices. The Parliament, it is strongly emphasized, may follow this constitutional route to set aside the practice of triple talaq. The court observes:

> We understand that it is not appropriate to tender advice to the legislature, to enact law on an issue. However, the position, as it presents in the present case, seems to be a little different. Herein, the views expressed by the rival parties are not in contradiction. The Union of India has appeared before us in support of the cause of the petitioners. The stance adopted by the Union of India is sufficient for us to assume, that the Union of India supports the petitioners' cause. Unfortunately, the Union seeks at our hands, what truly falls in its own.[10]

The third argument underlines the most interesting aspect of the triple talaq controversy. The court finds that all stakeholders—the women petitioners, the government and the AIMPLB—agree that the practice of triple talaq is a social evil and must be stopped. However, they propose different possible routes to get rid of this perverted custom.

The government and the main petitioners in the case claimed that that this practice should be banned by the judiciary. The AIMPLB, on the other hand, questioned the judicial intervention and asserted that triple talaq, being a social problem, should be resolved by the Muslims themselves. The court recognizes the merit of these two conflicting claims for making a crucial distinction between the problem and the proposed solutions. Invoking the 'advisory' submitted by the AIMPLB as evidence to show its commitment for eradicating triple talaq (see Box 1 on the following page), the court observes:

A perusal of the above affidavit reveals, that the AIMPLB has undertaken to issue an advisory through its website, to advise those who enter into a matrimonial alliance, to agree in the nikahnama, that their marriage would not be dissolvable by 'talaq-e-biddat'. The AIMPLB has sworn an affidavit to prescribe guidelines, to be followed in matters of divorce, emphasizing that 'talaq-e-biddat' be avoided. It would not be incorrect to assume, that even the AIMPLB is on board, to assuage the petitioner's cause.[11]

Keeping this broad consensus in mind, the court proposes two practical solutions: (a) The Parliament should make a law to ban triple talaq within a period of six months and (b) Until the law is passed, triple talaq as a practice must be treated as legally invalid. It is stated:

Till such time as legislation in the matter is considered, we are satisfied in injuncting Muslim husbands, from pronouncing 'talaq-e-biddat' as a means for severing their matrimonial relationship. The instant injunction, shall in the first instance, be operative for a period of six months. If the legislative process commences before the expiry of the period of six months, and a positive decision emerges towards redefining 'talaq-e-biddat' (three pronouncements of 'talaq', at one and the same time)—as one, or alternatively, if it is decided that the practice of 'talaq-e-biddat' be done away with altogether, the injunction would continue, till legislation is finally enacted. Failing which, the injunction shall cease to operate.[12]

Box 1: Affidavit submitted by the AIMPLB

'I am the Secretary of All India Muslim Personal Board will issue an advisory through its Website, Publications and Social Media Platforms and thereby advise the persons who perform 'Nikah' (marriage) and request them to do the following:- (a) At the time of performing 'Nikah' (marriage), the person performing the 'Nikah' will advise the Bridegroom/Man that in case of differences leading to Talaq, the Bridegroom/Man shall not pronounce three divorces in one sitting since it is an undesirable practice in shariat; (b) That at the time of performing 'Nikah' (Marriage), the person performing the 'Nikah' will advise both the Bridegroom/Man and the Bride/Woman to incorporate a condition in the 'Nikahnama' to exclude resorting to pronouncement of three divorces by her husband in one sitting.

I say and submit that, in addition, the Board is placing on record, that the Working Committee of the Board had earlier already passed certain resolutions in the meeting held on 15th & 16th April, 2017 in relation to Divorce (Talaq) in the Muslim community. Thereby it was resolved to convey a code of conduct/guidelines to be followed in the matters of divorce particularly emphasizing to avoid pronouncement of three divorces in one sitting. A copy of the resolution dated April 16, 2017 along with the relevant Translation of Resolution Nos. 2, 3, 4 & 5 relating to Talaq (Divorce) is enclosed herewith for the perusal of this Hon'ble Court and marked as Annexure A-1 (Colly) [Page Nos. 4 to 12] to the present Affidavit.'

The reception to the judgement was very interesting. Despite the fact that triple talaq as a practice had been banned by the judiciary, the AIMPLB welcomed the verdict. The official statement issued by the board said, 'The judgement vindicates our stand and ensures the fundamental right of citizens of this country to freely profess and practise their religious faith/beliefs.'[13]

This overtly positive reading actually underlined the nature of AIMPLB's politics. The public image of the board as a representative body of Muslims is legitimized by the court. In such a scenario, the judgement is seen as favourable and supportive. Since the court has asked the Parliament to make a new law considering the claims of all the stakeholders, there is a possibility for the AIMPLB to reclaim its status as the apex Muslim religious organization. If the AIMBLB is invited to participate in the deliberation on the proposed new law (the way it happened in 1985 during the Shah Bano case), the conservative ulema would be able to secure their lost legitimacy as Muslim representatives.

The BMMA's strident opposition to triple talaq and the UCC also find resonance in this ruling. The court has asked the Parliament to make a Muslim divorce law, and the issue of the UCC is clearly separated from it. This legal clarity is actually employed by the BMMA to make a case for a progressive Muslim family law. In a public letter, the BMMA makes it clear that the judgement is not an end in itself. It is argued:

The Supreme Court setting aside triple talaq in its judgement [. . .] was a historical step forward in Muslim women's struggle for gender justice in marriage and family matters [. . .] The Parliament must live up to its duty of passing a Muslim Family Law just as they passed the Hindu Marriage Act, 1955 and Hindu Succession Act, 1956. Justice for Indian Muslim women can be enabled either through amendments to the Shariat Application Act, 1937 as well as the Dissolution of Muslim Marriages Act, 1939 or a completely new enactment of Muslim personal law. BMMA has [. . .] prepared a draft Muslim Family Law based on Quranic tenets concerning age of marriage, mehr, talaq, polygamy, maintenance, custody of children, etc. These are in consonance with the Constitution of India. This government must now listen to the voices of progressive Muslim women [. . .] the government and [the] Opposition [must] stop politicizing the issue and ensure a balanced and comprehensive law.[14]

The most enthusiastic response to the judgement came from the government. The government welcomed the judgement and assured Muslim women that a new law would be enacted to ban triple talaq. Following this commitment, the Muslim Women (Protection of Rights on Marriage) Bill, 2017, was introduced in the Lok Sabha in December 2017. The statement of object of the bill says:

In spite of the Supreme Court setting aside talaq-e-biddat, and the assurance of AIMPLB, there have been reports of divorce by way of talaq-e-biddat from different parts of the country. It is seen that setting aside talaq-e-biddat by the Supreme Court has not worked as any deterrent in bringing down the number of divorces by this practice among certain Muslims. It is, therefore, felt that there is a need for State action to give effect to the order of the Supreme Court and to redress the grievances of victims of illegal divorce.[15]

Box 2: What is the Shah Bano case?

Shah Bano, a sixty-two-year-old Muslim woman and mother of five, was divorced by her husband, a lawyer, Mohammad Ahmad Khan, in 1978. She filed a case against her ex-husband for maintenance (AIR 1985 SC 945). In 1985, the Supreme Court ruled in her favour and underlined the need for a common civil law in the country. The Supreme Court held that if the divorced wife is able to maintain herself, the husband's liability ceases with the expiration of the period of iddat, but if she is unable to maintain herself after the period of iddat, she is entitled to have recourse to Section 125 of the Code of Criminal Procedure. This judgement created a stir in the country. The AIMPLB and other Muslim organizations launched a nationwide agitation against the Supreme Court ruling and the protection of Muslim personal law and shariat. Finally, the then Rajiv Gandhi government introduced a bill in the Parliament against this judgement. The new law, the Muslim Women (Protection of Rights on Divorce) Act, 1986, overturned the Supreme Court verdict.

Let's punish Muslim men!

It is important to note that the Supreme Court judgement does not clarify the nature of offence if triple talaq is practised by a man. However, the 2017 bill proposed to make the declaration of talaq a cognizable and non-bailable crime. It is important to note that in the case of a cognizable offence, a police officer may arrest an accused person without any warrant.

Hence, if a husband is alleged to have pronounced triple talaq, he may be arrested by the police. Furthermore, the husband can be imprisoned for up to three years along with a fine. The Muslim woman, against whom talaq is practised, is given a right to claim subsistence allowance from her husband for herself and her dependant children. This allowance will be decided by a first-class magistrate. The woman is also entitled to seek custody of her minor children.

The Congress supported the bill with a few amendments. However, it was severely opposed by the Opposition parties, such as the RJD, the All India Itehadul Muslimeen, the Biju Janata Dal, the AIADMK and the Indian Union Muslim League. The Lok Sabha passed the bill on 28 December 2017.

The debate on the bill introduces us to a few inherent technical problems. Two important issues need to be underlined here. First, it is clear from the Supreme Court judgement that if a person pronounces the word 'talaq' three times with an intention to divorce his wife, it would not affect the status of the marriage. It means they would remain husband and wife in legal terms.

But the bill intends to make the uttering of the word 'talaq' a punishable offence, for which a Muslim man may receive a jail term. The question arises: If the marriage, as a civic contract, cannot be broken by the husband even though he says talaq three times, how could this act be treated as a non-bailable crime strictly in legal terms? This is what Sushmita Dev said in the debate on the bill in the Lok Sabha:

This Bill is effectively bringing a matter like divorce, which is generally in the domain of civil jurisdiction, into the domain of criminal jurisdiction. That means, now, it is going to be a criminal offence and the logic behind that, as per the Statement of Objects and Reasons, is that it will act as a deterrent [. . .] if you make it a cognizable offence and a non-bailable offence and you are giving women the right of subsistence allowance, how she will ensure she gets this subsistence allowance and who is going to give it to her [. . .] When you criminalize something like this, will it alienate the Muslim community more than it already has? [. . .] Will you [. . .] ensure that this bill will not open up abuse of this law against Muslim men in the country in the name of protecting Muslim women?[16]

Secondly, the bill is based on the premise that Muslims constitute a single religious community and the practice of triple talaq is the only social problem they face. Unlike the Supreme Court judgement, the bill does not clarify that the custom of triple talaq is prevalent only among the Hanafi Sunni Muslims.

The government did not wait for the approval of the Rajya Sabha and promulgated the Muslim Women (Protection of Rights on Marriage) Ordinance, 2018, on 19 September 2018. The ordinance, as expected, relied entirely on the draft bill presented by the government in the Lok Sabha. Defining triple talaq as a cognizable offence, the ordinance upholds the provision that the accused may get up to three years imprisonment, with a fine.

Nevertheless, the ordinance has three specific features. First, in order to qualify the nature of triple talaq as a punishable act, it makes a few new provisions. Triple talaq will only be recognized as a cognizable offence if information about it is given by the woman against whom talaq is practised. Moreover, if the pronouncement of talaq is reported by any person related to the women by blood or marriage, that would also be considered an offence.[17] Second, the accused husband may be granted bail. However, it depends on the discretion of the magistrate. If the woman agrees and the magistrate is satisfied, a person accused of triple talaq may be release on parole.[18] Third, if the woman is of the opinion that the offence of triple talaq may not happen in the future, she may approach the court to stop legal proceedings and settle the dispute. However, the terms and conditions of this dispute resolution will only be determined by the magistrate.[19]

It is obvious that the recent legislative initiatives to ban triple talaq—the bill and the ordinance—are full of contradictions.

Apart from the legal inconsistencies, these moves clearly reaffirm the assumptions about Muslims, which we have noted in the first section. Let us conclude this chapter by highlighting two aspects of the politics of triple talaq.

First, the manner in which Muslim men are envisaged in these debates is highly problematic. The government seems to endorse the view that the protection of the rights of Muslim women can only be possible if Muslim men are punished—as if Muslim women do not consider themselves Muslims at all and their only objective is to protect their marriages! The issues raised by the BMMA and other Muslim women organizations, such as the economic empowerment of women and having an egalitarian and gender-just Islamic family law in India, are virtually ignored.

Second, the government has given a new lease of life to the ulema class in the country in a very interesting manner. Unlike the Rajiv Gandhi government, which relied entirely on the AIMPLB for drafting the Muslim Women (Protection of Rights on Divorce) Act, 1986, the Modi government is very critical of the Muslim religious elite. However, the negative image of the AIMPLB has been tactically used to publicize the positive attitude of the government towards Muslim women. This undue recognition given to the AIMPLB has strengthened the media perception of Islamic clergy. The ulema have successfully carved out a space for themselves as decisive interpreters of religious texts.

8

The New Muslim Elite

Thinking the unthinkable!

> I wanted a role for myself in politics . . . I approached a few political parties, including the Congress. I met some senior party leaders. I was thoroughly disillusioned: Missing was the dynamism and a sense of direction. There was little there except lust of power. And then the unthinkable happened. I had a chance meeting with Modi. He greeted me warmly and invited me to join him if I was interested in his project of nation-building.[1]

These were the sentiments expressed by Syed Zafar Islam in an article titled 'A Birthday Card to the PM'. Islam explains the causes that led him to join Modi's BJP—a party which is often projected as being anti-Muslim. His narrative of struggle, however, is slightly different.

He tells us that after spending considerable time in the Aligarh Muslim University (AMU) and IIM Ahmedabad as a student, he worked in the financial sector. He went on to become a managing director with Deutsche Bank. This successful career in the banking sector did not satisfy him. As a politically conscious Muslim individual, Islam approached many political parties to carve out a meaningful space for himself in politics. According to him, the so-called netas disillusioned him completely.

And, finally, as he puts it, 'the unthinkable happened'—he met Narendra Modi! Islam found a great dynamism in Modi. He also realized there were a number of remarkable similarities he shared with him—they both came from humble backgrounds, had struggled a lot and both of them had 'a sense of direction'.

And the rest, as they say, is history. Islam is one of the national spokespersons of the BJP today.

Islam's self-portrayal as a pro-Modi Muslim representative certainly reflects a few political necessities, which virtually all BJP leaders adhere to these days. However, there is an element of truth in his story. He represents an aspirational member of the Muslim middle class—a product of the post-1990 liberalization era—who is not satisfied with the existing forms of Islamic religiosities as well as the established idioms of Muslim politics. The presence of this aspirational class of Muslims has not yet been recognized in public discourse, but its increasing influence on contemporary Muslim politics cannot be underestimated.

Terms such as 'Muslim middle class' or 'Muslim elites' somehow go against the present-day sense of political correctness. We are forced to imagine Indian Muslims either as victims or as a global threat to the nation.

The narrative of Muslim victimhood, which emerged as an official explanation after the publication of the Sachar report, is invoked by the so-called secular elite to represent themselves as guardians of Muslim interests.[2] On the other hand, Hindutva politics relies on global Islamic terrorism to present India's Muslims as a potential threat. The class distinction among Muslims is not in the least bit important for them.

These contradictory depictions of Muslims in India do not allow us to pay close attention to the internal configuration of

Muslim communities, especially the formation of a new middle class. This chapter tries to address this intellectual apathy by asking two specific questions. First, is it possible to think of a class among the Muslims of India purely in economic terms? Second, how does this class influence Muslim identity in general and Muslim politics in particular?

The Muslim class structure

Pioneering research conducted by Sanjeer Alam introduces us to the complex economic profile of Muslims in contemporary India. His findings are based on the National Sample Survey (NSS) that collects information, among other things, on the educational status of individuals and their employment situation.[3] On the basis of this analysis, three features of the Muslim class structure may be identified.

First, it is found that that globalization has not yet fully restructured class configuration among Muslims in India. The majority of Muslims either work as casual workers or they are engaged in self-employment. Only a few Muslims (around 19 per cent) are engaged in what are called regular salaried jobs. Although this economic unevenness is not entirely specific to Muslims (among the SCs/STs, the proportion of casual workers is very high in comparison to those holding regular salaried jobs), liberalization has affected them most. This is what the Sachar Committee also identifies. The report notes:

Displacement from traditional occupations has contributed to Muslims being deprived of their means of livelihood and has led to economic backwardness. Despite the economic boom being talked about in India, today one finds that Muslims in India have had to bear the brunt of the so called 'competitive' forces unleashed by liberalization. Internal and external liberalization has brought with it considerable costs in terms of unemployment and displacement of workers who have lost their jobs to competitive companies that import products. Muslims, by and large, are engaged in the unorganized sector of the economy which rarely enjoys protection of any kind and therefore the adverse impact of liberalization has been more acute for them. The traditional occupations of Muslims, in industries such as silk and sericulture, hand and power looms, the leather industry, automobile repairing, garment making, have borne the brunt of liberalization [. . .] The artisans that survive have to face problems related to infrastructure (e.g., expensive power), expensive raw materials (due to lack of subsidies), and non-availability of credit and absence of marketing support.[4]

However, the process of globalization can also be interpreted very differently. It is also possible to infer from the same set of data that the above-mentioned 19 per cent of Muslims, who earn regular salaries, are in an advantageous position in comparison to poor, self-employed Muslims and casual workers. In such a scenario, one needs to unpack the category of 'salaried class' to avoid simplistic conclusions. After all, 'regular salary' does not necessarily contribute to the economic upward mobility of an individual. There is a possibility that a self-employed person may earn more than a salaried person.

So now let us examine the second feature of the Muslim class structure. The salaried job may be classified into white-collar jobs and other jobs. (This classification is not entirely arbitrary, the NSS also uses it.) Certain positions held—such as managers, executives, technical and other professionals, administrators, teachers, clerks—may be treated as white-collar jobs. These forms of employment signify the relatively higher earnings of an individual as well as his/her social status as part of the educated elite.

NSSO data shows that Muslims face disadvantages in accessing white-collar occupations. Even educated Muslims find it difficult to utilize their degrees in the job market. Yet, around 6 per cent of the total Muslim male workforce (aged twenty-five to sixty years) manages to enter into this elite class. The standard definition of Muslim marginalization does not apply to them simply because of their class background. Interestingly, caste differences among these educated, white-collar job-holding Muslims is rather insignificant—more than half of them come from upper castes, while the rest belong to Muslim OBCs.

Muslim presence in the banking sector is a good example to substantiate this point. In a recent study, it has been found that Muslims constitute around 3 per cent of the directors and senior executives—sixty-two of the 2324 executives—among the BSE 500 companies.[5] Obviously, this number may be used to underline the marginalization of Muslims. But this also reflects a kind of serious class disparity between common Muslims and the Muslim economic elite.

And this brings us to the third feature of the Muslim class structure. There is a minority of Muslim businessmen, landowners and traders who still have an important role to play in the internal makings of the power hierarchy. Although we do not have adequate data or any systematic study to demonstrate the exact status of this economic class, the extraordinary class divides among Muslims across the country is self-evident.

Table 1: Occupational distribution by socio-religious communities, 2011–12

Socio-religious communities	Occupation			
	Casual labourer	Self-employed	Regular salaried	All
Scheduled Tribes	37.6	50.0	12.4	100
Scheduled Castes	48.7	32.6	18.7	100
OBCs (Hindus)	24.4	51.6	20.0	100
Forward castes (Hindus)	13.2	53.4	33.4	100
Muslims (OBCs)	32.6	48.9	18.5	100
Muslims (Gen.)	26.6	54.9	18.5	100
Others	17.4	53.0	29.6	100
Overall	29.6	48.3	22.0	100

Source: Sanjeer Alam's calculation from the raw data file of the National Sample Survey, 68th Round, 2011–12 (Alam, 2016)
Note: Figures pertain to male workers aged 25–50 years

Table 2: Educational attainment and access to white-collar jobs by socio-religious communities (2011–12)

Socio-religious communities	% Share in worker population (Male)	% Share in workers with graduation and above (Male)	% Share in white-collar workers (Male)	Ratio of share in white-collar jobs to share in workers' education up to secondary school and above (Col. 5/4)
1	2	3	4	5
Scheduled Tribes	8.5	4.1	3.5	0.85
Scheduled Castes	18.5	9.5	8.9	0.93
OBC (Hindus)	36.3	30.9	28.6	0.92
Forward castes (Hindus)	21.5	44.6	47.6	1.06
Muslims (OBC)	6.1	2.6	2.1	0.80
Muslims (Gen.)	6.2	3.8	3.7	0.97
Others	2.7	4.5	5.2	1.24
	100	100	100	

Source: Sanjeer Alam's calculation from the raw data file of the National Sample Survey, 68th Round, 2011–12 (Alam 2016)
Note: Figures pertain to individuals aged 25–50 years

Who is the Muslim elite?

On the basis of this discussion, the Muslim community of India may be divided into three categories:

- Poor and lower middle-class Muslims
- The emerging Muslim professional elite
- Traditional Muslim upper-class elite

This classification, however, requires some refinement. Two important points need to be remembered here.

First, the class status of rich and prosperous Muslims does not always function as a self-governing mechanism that leads them to take up the role of Muslims leaders. There are many rich and economically well-off Muslim individuals who do not show any interest in the social welfare of the Muslim community in general and Muslim politics in particular. Hence, presuming that rich Muslims would eventually operate as a dominant Muslim stakeholder is a highly misleading assumption. Although the economic background of an individual does affect his/her prospects as a member of the community elite, bearing in mind the distinction between those rich and powerful Muslims who prefer to join public life as Muslim figures and those affluent members of the Muslim community who continue to operate in the realms of their professional world is very important.

Muslim public figures—MLA, MPs, the ulema, professionals and even those who participate in prime-time TV shows as Muslim representatives—actually work as 'organic intellectuals' in this framework. They offer meanings to frequently used terms related to Muslims, define various expressions of Muslimness and make statements about Muslim views and public opinion. Their own vested interests as a class gets amalgamated and refined in this process and equips them to make broad observations about

Muslims or a section of Muslims as a homogeneous class. In my view, this group of Muslims may legitimately be called the 'Muslim elite'.

Rich and powerful Muslims, who do not make any claim to represent Muslims, also extract a symbolic value. Muslim businessmen, economically powerful farmers and landowners, film stars, civil servants, university teachers and media personalities are often counted as numbers in their respective professions to measure Muslim presence in various institutions. Many a time, this Muslim presence is misleadingly understood as a form of Muslim representation. This confusion between Muslim presence and the claims of Muslim representation produce various kinds of strange public debates.

The controversy around Aamir Khan's statements, that his wife does not feel secure in present-day India, is a good example. In an interview in November 2015, Khan said:

> [Wife] Kiran and I have lived all our lives in India. For the first time, she said, should we move out of India? That's a disastrous and big statement for Kiran to make to me. She fears for her child. She fears about what the atmosphere around us will be. She feels scared to open the newspapers every day. That does indicate that there is a sense of growing disquiet.[6]

This statement was widely debated. What was remarkable in the debate was Khan's Muslim identity. A case was registered against him for showing disrespect towards the fundamental duties enlisted in the Indian Constitution.[7] Many BJP–Hindutva supporters argued that Aamir Khan must remember that this country (Hindus!) has given him credibility as an actor and, therefore, his statement is 'anti-national' in nature. Khan was not invoking his Muslim identity in this case; even his so-called controversial statement is based on an observation by his wife, who is Hindu!

Why is Aamir Khan recognized as a Muslim (and not as an Indian citizen) in this case, despite the fact that he does not claim to represent the Muslims of India?

It is true that Aamir Khan does not represent Muslims; yet, his Muslim name is always reckoned to assess Muslim presence in the Indian film industry. By this logic, Khan, being an affluent person with a Muslim name, cannot be called Muslim elite—partly because of his strident refusal to speak as a Muslim and partly because of his professional identity as an actor and Bollywood celebrity.

The recent tolerance/intolerance controversy also introduces us to the second point about the relationship between one's economic class and his/her status as a member of the Muslim elite. It is often argued the internal class/caste differentiations among Muslims evaporate at the time of communal violence. Rich as well as poor Muslims are attacked and killed indiscriminately.

There is an element of truth in this argument. The manner in which Ehsan Jafri—a rich and powerful Muslim, an ex-MP from Gujarat and someone who had access to the top political leaders of the country—was killed during the 2002 Gujarat riots, shows that class and elite status becomes irrelevant when Muslims are identified only as Muslims.[8]

The question arises: How is one's elite position produced and reproduced in such contexts?

It is important to remember that the Muslim elite—rich and powerful Muslims who participate in public discussions and debates as Muslims—have to adjust themselves in the dominant discourse of politics. Their idioms, metaphors and political vocabulary evolve out of the public environment.

For instance, Hindutva is the dominant discourse at the moment, which cannot be ignored by political players. The Muslim elite also respond to it in a number of ways. A section of the elite oppose Hindutva to assert their legitimacy as critical–secular Muslims, while there are Muslims who embrace Hindutva wholeheartedly in the name of protecting the interests of the community. In both cases, Hindutva is reproduced and sustained!

These contextual responses of the Muslim elite, in any case, cannot guarantee that Hindutva's anti-Muslim rhetoric will not take a violent form, even against those Muslims who are in their good books. In fact, it all depends on political–ideological requirements. If Hindu consolidation is to be achieved through negotiations, Hindutva would prefer a 'good Muslims versus the bad Muslims' formula and create a pool of its favourable Muslim leaders. However, if the objective is to create a Hindu impact to demonstrate the anger and assertion of Hindu pride, the 'Muslim action–Hindu reaction' theory would be the favoured mode of political action. The demolition of Babri Masjid and the 2002 Gujarat riots are examples of this latter form.

Let us summarize this discussion to propose a workable conceptualization of the Muslim elite.

The Muslim elites are a class of economically rich, religiously dominant, politically influential and culturally powerful Muslims who articulate Muslim views on relevant issues and debates and seek legitimacy as representatives.

'A class for itself'

For the sake of analysis, I find four interesting characteristics of the contemporary Muslim elite—its self-perception as a class, its imagination of Indian Islam, its caste background and its political openness.

We must note that the Muslim elite is not at all homogeneous. They come from different regions; they are involved in different professions; and the cultural capital they invest in public life is also different in nature.

For instance, the new middle class of Muslim professionals consists of semi-urban and urban-educated Muslim professionals and upwardly mobile, semi-rural elites. Unlike the Muslim elites of the 1960s and 1970s, who came primarily from erstwhile Muslim-dominated urban centres like Hyderabad, Lucknow and Delhi, these new Muslim professionals belong to lower-middle-class Muslim neighbourhoods in metro cities, small towns and *kasbas*.

Delhi's Zakir Nagar, Mumbai's Byculla, Hyderabad's old city, Kochi, Ranchi and other small towns with Muslim concentrations are the places gradually producing an upwardly mobile set of Muslim individuals.

This regional diversity functions in an interesting way. While these professionals continue to operate in their own specific areas of work, the aspiration to move forward transforms them from a 'class in itself' to 'a class for itself'.

As a class in itself, these Muslims transcend the economic class they once belonged to and place themselves in a relatively higher economic strata. This change of class also brings in a realization that they are the obvious leaders of the poor, marginalized Indian Muslim community. This self-consciousness transforms them into a class for itself—a class which recognizes its location and its interests. Two examples are crucial to elaborate this point.

Nagpur-based Indian Muslim Chamber of Commerce and Industry (IMCCI) is a professional body that caters to the needs of Muslim businessmen.[9] One of the stated objectives of the IMCCI is to function as a commercial bridge between various businesses both domestically and globally for strengthening the economy through mutually beneficial trade and investment.[10] The organization strongly supports foreign direct investment (FDI) in India. Its global vision says:

Diverse types of FDI lead to diverse types of spillovers, skill transfers and physical capital flows. It enhances the chances of developing [an] internationally competitive business environment. It is observed that FDI plays a positive role in enhancing the economic growth of the host and home country as well. Taking all above mention observation [sic] into consideration, we, in IMCCI, very much promote foreign investment into India through us which is beneficial to grow our members' business as well as to grow the economy of the nation.[11]

This overwhelming support for liberalization, particularly for FDI in all sectors, simply goes against the views and perceptions of the Muslim lower classes about the impact of globalization, especially with regard to small-scale units. As a professional body which protects the interests of their members, the IMCCI does not show any interest in these kinds of Muslim anxieties.

The Association of Muslim Professionals (AMP), a Mumbai-based organization, however, responds to Muslim marginalization in a different way. The AMP describes itself as a 'platform for all Muslim professionals [. . .] to share their knowledge, intellect, experience and skills for the overall development of the Muslim Community.'[12] This organization is led mainly by Muslim businessmen and white-collar professionals. The AMP has the following stated objectives:

- To bring together Muslims from all walks of life to interact and co-operate with an objective to educate, motivate, organize and inspire.
- To join hands in order to eradicate evil practices from our society which lead to untold miseries.
- To see that the community puts its unspent energy to constructive use.
- To instil a feeling of confidence among our younger generation.

- To play a leading and active role in the development and transformation of Muslims into a responsible community, consolidating a stronger place for ourselves in Indian society and the global arena at large.[13]

These objectives adhere to the popular Muslim victimhood story. Although the AMP works on a number of projects, which they describe as 'Muslim empowerment', their position on the impact of economic liberalization on Muslims and issues concerning Muslim agricultural labourers are not at all clear. Class disparity among Muslims is completely missing in this imagination of the Muslim community.

The layered management of Islam is the second unique feature of the contemporary Muslim elite. The conventional binary between practising mullah-type Muslims and the self-declared secular/liberal/cultural Muslims has become rather irreverent. Although there are individuals who take extreme essentialist positions either in supporting Islam or in rejecting it completely, the intensity of such provocative debates among the Muslim elite has considerably decreased.

Liberal Muslims who do not practise Islam as a religion and describe themselves as atheists or culturally active Muslims, do not make offensive comments on the practice of religion per se. Likewise, the ulema elite do not overemphasize religion. As a result, an interesting imagination of privatized Islam has evolved over the years. The Muslim elite keep Islam a 'private affair' by creating a thin line between public life and religious obligations.

This privatization fits well with the emerging form of Islamic religiosities, which advocates a policy of non-intervention in professional worldly affairs. The Tablighi Jamaat—which has become the dominant form of Sunni Islam in contemporary India—is a good example of this privatization of religion. (We have already discussed the nature of this kind of Islam in detail in the previous chapters.) This is precisely what Zafar Sareshwala, a highly successful Gujarati businessman and staunch supporter of Narendra Modi (until recently!), says:

> My physical appearance and 'image' is that of a stereotypical Muslim. I have a beard, my wife wears a burkha, we pray five times a day, we've done Hajj and we follow every Islamic tradition. But our views are enlightened precisely because we take the teachings of Islam seriously.[14]

The caste profile of the Muslim elite is the third determining characteristic. We have observed in previous chapters that the caste-based social stratification among Muslims has played an important role in the configuration of economic and political power at various levels. This is also true about the formation of the elite in contemporary India.

We find that upper-caste Ashrafs still constitute the majority of the Muslim elite. Yet, the rise of Muslim middle castes in various regions of the country cannot be underestimated. This phenomenon may reshape the sociological profile of the Muslim elite in the long run.

This is not at all surprising. As per official estimates quoted by the Sachar report, around 40 per cent of Muslims in India belong to the OBC category.[15] The upward mobility, educational empowerment and caste-consciousness of these Muslim OBCs— many of whom describe themselves as Pasmandas—is certainly going to affect the circulation of the Muslim elite. In the chapter on Muslim backwardness, we also found that two leading Pasmanda leaders from Bihar—Ejaz Ali and Ali Anwar Ansari—eventually became MPs in the Rajya Sabha. This political recognition as leaders of the Muslim Pasmanda communities has certainly affected the formation of the Muslim elite.

Political openness is the fourth characteristic of the contemporary Muslim elite. It would be completely inappropriate to think that the Muslim elite, despite being a class in itself, adheres to any one political ideology. There are three norms of Muslim politics which they have to follow.

First, they have to explicitly express their adherence to the Indian Constitution. This helps them to articulate their demands in the language of the law. The second norm follows from this legal commitment. They have to situate themselves in the realm of 'minority rights', which offers Muslims a legitimate legal identity. We have discussed this aspect in the previous chapter. Finally, they have to invoke 'Muslim contribution' and 'loyalty to nation' so as to legitimize their status as a stakeholder. We shall discuss these norms in the final chapter of this book. Here, suffice it to say that these unwritten norms actually set the terms of Muslim politics as a discourse.

It is clear that these three norms are open to various interpretations. For example, the legal-constitutionalism and minority rights are interpreted as justifications for the inclusion of Dalit Muslims in the SC list by the Pasmanda elite. But it does not stop the Muslim elite of the BJP to reject this demand, arguing that Muslim reservation goes against the very premise of secularism envisaged by the Constitution itself!

This relative openness offers them an opportunity to make conscious political choices towards identifying appropriate/ beneficial locations for them in the overall structure of power.

The politics, in this framework, is envisaged as an instrument to maximize individual as well as collective interest. Syed Zafar Islam's context-driven decision to join the BJP without asking for a ticket to contest elections, or Zafar Sareshwala's overwhelming support for Modi without giving up his Islamic identity are some of the revealing examples that demonstrate the political flexibility of the Muslim elite. In such cases, political idioms, such as secular/communal, national/anti-national and Muslim as victim/Muslims as a threat are not taken as the governing principles of politics. Instead, preference is given to practical, context-specific moves.

PART III

THE POLITICS OF SIYASI MUSLIMS

9

The Metaphors of Muslim Politics: Vote Bank, Good Muslims/Bad Muslims and Muslim Appeasement

Addressing a public meeting to mark the birth anniversary of BJS leader Deen Dayal Upadhyaya, Modi said:

> Our founding fathers have laid down the principles for us to follow. It is our duty to bring policies for the development of all the sections of the society [. . .] vote-bank politics is eating away our country like termites. Saving the country from vote-bank politics and its collateral damage is the objective of [the] BJP. Those promoting vote-bank politics did not care about that development.[1]

This was not the first time when Modi, like other BJP leaders, invoked the term 'vote bank' to criticize the policies, programmes and actions of non-BJP political parties. Making this differentiation more accurate and precise, Modi used another term—'development', which is introduced as an antithesis to the vote bank. Although the meanings of the terms 'vote bank' and/or 'development' are not elaborated upon in the speech, Modi was able to make his point. He was certainly referring to the electoral behaviour of Muslims of India, which, in his imagination of 'Sabka Saath, Sabka Vikas', had to be condemned in order to achieve progress.

Modi, however, must not be blamed for using ambiguous, vague and unclear expressions to outline the distinctiveness of his party. The idea of the 'Muslim vote bank' has never been defined in public discourses! Instead, two very different sets of conflicting arguments are given.

It is claimed that the 'Muslim vote' is very decisive in electoral politics because the 'winnability' of a candidate at the constituency level and the sustainability of any political coalition at the regional/ national level are inextricably associated with Muslim electoral support. The Muslim vote bank, in this framework, refers to the collective political strength of Muslim electorates.

The second argument is negative in nature. It is based on an assertion that Muslims have been used as a political commodity in the market of elections, especially by the secular parties. The BJP is the only political party which does not address Muslims as a vote bank, and that's the reason why the BJP does not promote tokenism in the name of Muslim appeasement.

Although these oversimplified and straightforward conclusions have been criticized as an imagined phenomenon, the Muslim vote bank seems to function as a dominant mode of explanation for interpreting Muslim engagements with electoral politics. This portrayal of Muslim politics is based on a strong conviction that the Muslims of India as a political community are fully conscious of their political interests and legal rights and, as a result, are sincerely involved in political action.

This assumption raises a few complicated questions:

- Does it mean that Muslim electoral politics could only be understood as the Muslim vote bank, which as a form of separatism simply goes against the collective national wisdom of politics as development/empowerment?

- Or does it mean that non-BJP political fronts do not have any conception of Muslim empowerment in the true sense of the term and are mainly engaged in nurturing vote-bank politics (or the Muslim vote bank), which eventfully destabilizes the pace of national growth?
- If this is the case, does it also mean that non-BJP political parties are involved in what is often called Muslim appeasement?
- Finally, do all Muslims believe in vote-bank politics? Or are there Muslims who oppose political separatism and believe in the development/empowerment of all? In other words, are there 'good Muslims' versus 'bad Muslims'?

These questions revolve around three key metaphors in Muslim politics: the Muslim vote bank, Muslim appeasement and good Muslims/bad Muslims. Interestingly, these metaphors are used as self-explanatory templates, as if the meanings of the terms vote bank, appeasement and good Muslims are fixed and defined. This may be the reason why we are often asked to take a clear-cut position with regard to them.

This chapter aims at explicating the changing meanings of these metaphors in postcolonial India by tracing the genealogy of the idea of the Muslim vote bank.

Vote banks as 'communities of voters'

The story of the term 'vote bank' is inextricably linked to the debate on the nature of Indian democracy itself, which began immediately after Independence. To understand the debate, we must first look at the institutional architecture of the election system in India.

The Constitution formally accepted the 'first past the post post' (FPTP) system of elections for the lower house of Parliament, known as the House of People and later as the Lok Sabha. All adult citizens (aged eighteen years or above) of the republic of India were given a right to vote for the first time. The entire country was also divided into electoral constituencies.

However, there were a few practical problems. It was found that the 1941 census was quite old for the purpose of designing the electoral constituencies for the first general election. To deal with this problem, the census commissioner was asked to prepare population estimates so that (a) A rational delimitation of all constituencies could be worked out and (b) Electoral constituencies could be divided into general seats and reserved seats for SC and ST communities.[2]

On the basis of these provisional estimates, electoral rolls were prepared and a total of 489 Lok Sabha constituencies were marked. To accommodate reserved seats (seventy-two seats were reserved for SC and twenty-seven for ST), three types of constituencies were also created:

- 314 single-member constituencies (where only one candidate, who would get the maximum numbers of votes polled, was to be declared as the winner).
- Eighty-six double-member constituencies (where there were two slots—one for general candidates and the other for SC and ST candidates. Each voter had two votes. The two candidates [one general and one from ST/ST] who would get the maximum numbers of votes polled were to be declared the winners).
- One three-member constituency (the seats where there were three slots—one general, one SC and one ST).[3]

Although it was a complicated system, there was an argument in favour of it. The political elite, especially the leaders of the Congress, were not keen on reviving the colonial electoral model based on the propositional representation on communal lines. This was one of the reasons why the reservation of seats for religious minorities in the lower house of Parliament was not accepted by the Constituent Assembly.

But the open competition based on the FPTP at the constituency level was also seen as a problematic proposal. This debate began in the early 1950s. A few senior socialist leaders, such as J.P. Narayan (popularly known as JP), forcefully argued that the parliamentary form of electoral democracy might not be suitable to achieve the goals of people's participation.

In a letter to Nehru, JP raised the issue of the multi-member constituency. He argued that the proposed Indian electoral system based on open competition would lead to centralization of power at the local level.

JP was particularly concerned about the exclusion of minorities. He suggested that every consistency should have three members, with a cumulative vote as the first choice.[4] This suggestion was based on the imagination that the single-member or even double-member constituencies cannot ensure real representation of the most marginalized members of society, who had not yet obtained individual citizenship rights so far.

However, Nehru was not in favour of these proposals. He defended the single-member constituency as the most effective mode of safeguarding the principles of democratic participation. Rejecting the proportional representation (PR) systems, he said:

> I could understand a complete system of proportional representation by a single transferable vote and plural constituencies. That is physically impossible as it is very intricate [. . .] If we introduced PR that would make it absolutely impossible, both from [the] organizational point of view, and [from] that of the voter, who will not understand its intricacies.[5]

In another letters, Nehru elaborated this idea. He says: 'Democracy originally was thought of in smaller terms and was presumably effective. I just do not know what our elections will lead us or the country to, but the simpler they are, the better.'[6]

Nehru's strong views on the FPTP received overwhelming support after the success of the 1952 elections. It not only gave him the confidence to argue that a parliamentary form of democracy was suitable for the country but also legitimized his assertion that the FPTP system of elections could be the most appropriate mode of determining the popular participation of voters in India.

These grand, idealistic observations of Nehru, however, do not entirely represent the changing nature of everyday politics in the 1950s. The traditional power structure at the constituency level amalgamated well with the requirement of electoral competition and led to the formation of a highly localized elite. This local elite began to function as a link between political parties and the voters. The creation of such vote banks was an important political phenomenon in the 1950s. I take two examples to elaborate this point.

Sociologist M.N. Srinivas conducted fieldwork-based research in a village called Rampura in the Mysore region (in Karnataka) in 1953. Srinivas discovered the existence of some patrons, mainly from the 'dominant castes', who worked as mediators between the political competitors and the voters. He writes:

A patron's following can be made to yield him economic and other benefits. Patrons from the dominant caste can secure a larger number of followers than patrons from non-dominant castes. The rural patrons are 'vote banks' for the politicians, and during elections they are approached for votes. In return, patrons expect favours—licenses for buses and rice-mills, and seats in medical and technological colleges for their kinsfolk. The existence of such links between patrons and politicians establishes a continuum between rural and urban forces, making each responsive.[7]

Srinivas also noted that the competitive politics of vote banks also strengthened the powers of dominant groups in the rural environment. He informed:

> The numerical strength of a caste influences its relations with the other castes. The capacity to muster a number of able-bodied men for a fight, and reputation for aggressiveness, are relevant factors. Considerations of power do prevail. The members of the non-dominant castes may be abused, beaten, grossly underpaid, or their women required to gratify the sexual desires of the powerful men in the dominant caste. The patrons from the dominant caste are 'vote banks' for the politicians.[8]

F.G. Bailey, sociologist and researcher, who did his fieldwork in rural Orissa (now Odisha) in the late 1950s, also found a similar kind of political manoeuvring by the rural elite. He, however, tells us another vote-bank story. According to Bailey:

> There [. . .] are small, tightly-knit caste associations, seldom extending to the width of even one constituency. These organizations have a council and leaders who lay down rules of ritual behaviour, settle marital disputes, hear cases of conduct considered prejudicial to the good name of the caste, and organize meetings and celebrations. These organizations sometimes have a strong sense of solidarity, and this, combined with the people's ignorance of what is at stake in an election, makes it possible for an astute candidate to gain the votes of the whole group merely by winning over its leaders. This is, in other words, a vote bank.[9]

This observation is slightly different from the Mysore case study. Here, a caste association is organizing itself not merely in cultural and sociological terms but also in direct political fashion. The notion of caste solidarity, in this sense, may also be seen as an outcome of electoral competitiveness. 'Vote bank', for

Bailey, therefore, symbolizes (a) The power of the caste elite to create solidarity in the group as committed voters and (b) The bargaining capabilities of the rural elite to work out favourable equations with political parties. This is exactly what political sociologist D.L. Sheth observed. He writes:

> Political parties and activists put a premium on the mechanisms of electioneering rather than on the discussion of critical issues, policy choice and problems of governmental performances. They [. . .] depend on 'local bosses' and 'miracle men' of the polls than on patient cultivation of voter support, based on the record of their work. Relying on vote banks and bargainers who are supposed to control the vote banks, they tend to extend the system of patronage and spoils. The voters, in turn, come to interpret elections as providing opportunities to extract individual and group benefits.[10]

It is worth mentioning that the use of the term 'vote bank' was not entirely restricted to serious academic discussions. JP's seminal essay titled *A Plea for Reconstruction of Indian Polity*, which was published in 1959, also underlined these anxieties at the national level. Although JP did not directly use the term 'vote bank' in this text, his description of the election process as an 'experience of demagoguery' in India is very illuminating. He says:

> The need to catch the votes create an unlimited opportunity for indulging in half-truths, even outright lies sometimes; for exciting passions, more often than not, the base passion; for arousing false hope by making dishonest but pleasing promises. Hardly any issue of public policy is presented to the people in its true light [. . .] In the short period of twelve years we have had sufficient experience of demagoguery and the harm it has done to the national interest.[11]

JP's observation adds another crucial dimension to the vote-bank idea. By describing the electoral process as demagoguery, he pinpoints the manipulative approach of the national political elite who actually fought elections in the name of nation-building and democracy.

JP seems to envisage the centralization of power, an outcome of vote-bank-based demagoguery, as a highly multilayered phenomenon. The rich and powerful caste/class leadership at the constituency level bargained with the politicians in the name of 'community interest'. This local elite employed the traditional solidarity and caste association to form a 'community of voters', who were used to make winnable coalitions at the local level.

On the other hand, political parties adjusted themselves to accommodate these localized vote banks. Poll promises were redefined, manifestos were carefully crafted and religious and caste factors were taken into consideration in distributing tickets. Consequently, a few favourable communities of committed voters at the national level emerged in the 1950s.

For instance, the Congress, being a coalition of different competing ideological and political interests, began to concentrate on upper-caste/class Hindus, Muslims and Harijan communities. The main Opposition parties, the communists and the socialists, focused entirely on the working-class communities and rural landless farmers; and the rightist parties, such as the Hindu Mahasabha and the BJS, tried to mobilize upper- and middle-caste Hindu and Punjabi communities, especially the refugees. In this context, the idea of the Muslim vote bank also emerged, sustained and survived.

What is the Muslim vote bank?

Muslims, like other social groups, also formed various communities of committed voters at constituency levels throughout the country. However, public perception about the Muslim communities of voters was very different from that of other social groups. The highly diversified Muslim communities of voters were not entirely seen as a localized trend. Instead, Muslim voting was interpreted in national terms. There were two specific reasons behind it.

First, the Partition and the creation of Pakistan created a lasting impact on postcolonial Muslim identity. Common Muslims were held responsible for political separatism and even for the partition of the country. Post-Partition violence also made it difficult for Muslims to participate in public life as full citizens. They were often asked to prove their nationalism and loyalty. In the backdrop of this anti-Muslim atmosphere, Muslim participation at various stages of political processes was recognized as a homogeneous, collective community response.

Secondly, 'Muslim isolation'—a term frequently used by Nehru to address Muslims—actually became a defining template of Muslim politics immediately after the Partition. Congress leaders, especially Nehru and Azad, used it to assure Muslims that their life and properties were secured in the republic of India; Hindu rightists used it to allege that Muslims had to give up their inward-looking Islamic attitude and participate in the national mainstream as Indianized Muslims; and the Muslim elites used it to bargain with the state on behalf of an isolated Muslim community. Two examples may be given here.

Writing to chief ministers in the early 1950s, Nehru wrote:

> We must also remember that Muslims are very poorly represented in our Services today, whether civil or police or military. They have thus a feeling of isolation. Many of our servicemen, however much they may try to be impartial, as they do, may still have some background of prejudice. Because of all this, state governments, district authorities and the police have always to remember this background and to keep wide awake.[12]

Nehru's use of the term 'Muslim isolation' has a double meaning. He is keen to transform public institutions into completely secular bodies; at the same time, he is also interested in encouraging Muslims to take active part in public life, without being communal.

His vision of 'nationalist apolitical Muslims' was not entirely imaginative. Jamiat-Ulama-e-Hind, a traditional collaborator of the Congress, decided to call itself an 'apolitical entity' immediately after the Partition. In its annual meeting on 19 April 1949, the Jamiat passed a resolution to 'concentrate on the religious and cultural uplift of the Muslim masses of India' as a non-political body. According to a newspaper report:

> Speakers supporting the resolution referred to the political role of the Jamiat for over a century and said that its object had been fulfilled after the achievement of freedom. The Jamiat should, therefore, centralize its activities in spheres other than politics. The policy resolution emphasized that Muslims should be persuaded to learn the Devanagari script, and pamphlets and booklets explaining the fundamental principles of Islam be published in both scripts, Devanagari and Urdu, for the development of better understanding among the Indian people. (Noorani, 2003, 79–80)

This 'apolitical' gesture of leading Muslim political organizations, especially with regard to so-called Muslim isolation in the 1950s, contributed significantly to the notion of the Muslim vote bank. The Muslim elite created an impression that the Muslims in India felt secluded after the creation of Pakistan and, therefore, there was a need to give voice to this voiceless community. Since they had already decided to give up politics in the electoral sense, it was easier for them to function as legitimate stakeholders of the Muslim community—at the local level as well as national level.

The outcome of such politics was predictable—political parties began to address Muslims as 'a national community of voters'. The creation of constituency-level Muslim coalitions was also seen as the local manifestation of national trends. The observation made by political scientist Rajni Kothari on Muslim electoral behaviour in the third and fourth general elections is an illuminating example. Kothari notes:

> Although there are no reserved seats for Muslims, by convention Congress and other major parties allot a certain minimum of their party tickets to the Muslims [. . .] Studies of electoral participation in constituencies with sizeable Muslim population also indicate a differentiated structure of support, fractional identities within the communities and coalition-making with other communities, in general as [a] process of secularization [. . .] and all without losing the distinctive Muslim identity.[13]

This observation must be seen in the backdrop of post-Nehru politics. Political developments in India in 1967, as various studies suggest, mark a deeper institutional crisis of the state. In order to deal with this crisis, particularly to reassert its institutional hegemony, the Indira Gandhi–led Congress government started encouraging controversial and disputed issues of religion and caste in an extraordinary way. Interestingly, established community institutions were disregarded and a few powerful individuals were recognized as representatives of various religious and caste communities by the state. Redefining the political system as a contested arena where the competing interests of various groups and identities could be reconciled, the government assumed ultimate responsibility to resolve these issues.

Muslims in this framework were also seen as a recognizable group who struggle to protect a few Muslim issues. This is exactly what Indira Gandhi had said. Addressing a public meeting in

Fatehgarh on 14 February 1974, she argued that if Muslims voted for the Muslim League or any other Muslim party, Hindu communal forces such as the BJS would be strengthened. In her opinion, 'Muslim League's tactics could only help the Jana Sangh and not the Muslims.' Muslim votes would be divided and help the BJS win the election in a triangular contest. Her resolve was simple: all Muslims must vote for the Congress in order to defeat the 'communal politics of Jana Sangh'.[14]

In order to consolidate Muslim votes, Indira Gandhi also encouraged what is often called 'fatwa politics'. The statement issued by Muslim leaders to support political parties were called political fatwas. It began in 1967, when the leading Islamic institution, the Deoband, issued official advice to Muslims to support the Congress in the Lok Sabha elections. However, it was Abdullah Bukhari, the imam of Jama Masjid, who legitimized fatwa politics in the 1970s and 1980s. In 1977, he supported the JP; in 1980, he campaigned for the Congress; in 1984, he was again with the Congress. The story of the imam's fatwa politics, interestingly, is absorbed in the narratives of communalism/ secularism in later years. Bukhari's claim to represent the political aspirations of India's Muslims was somehow accepted uncritically in popular political discourse.[15] We shall discuss this point in the next section of this book.

Let us conclude by identifying the three key elements of the Muslim vote bank:

1. **Muslims as a 'defined national community of voters':** The formation of communities of voters at the constituency level is an important aspect of Indian electoral politics. Muslim communities also form localized caste/biradari-based coalitions for electoral purposes. The Muslim communities of voters, however, are always imagined as a homogeneous national political entity. All political parties subscribe to

this position. Even the BJP (which argues for 'secularism of equality' and opposes special privileges given to religious minorities) and communist parties (which used to believe in the centrality of class thesis!) tend to define Muslims as a closed community of voters.

2. **A package called 'Muslim issues':** It is established that there are a few, specific, all-India Muslim issues, which can either be transformed into electoral promises or denied as Muslim appeasement. This formulation has evolved gradually over the years. Nehru's reassurance to Muslims that they were legitimate political stakeholders in India in the mid-1950s; the appeal of non-Congress parties, including the BJS (the predecessor of the BJP) to create a social alliance of Muslim Dalits and backward Muslims in the name of anti-Congressism in the late 1960s and early 1970s; the rise of a 'secular camp' in the wake of the Shah Bano and Babri Masjid controversies in the late 1980s and 1990s; and finally the proposal for Muslim reservation by UPA 1 and 2 have contributed to the making of a few Muslim issues.

3. **Muslims always vote for Muslim issues:** It is asserted that the Muslims of India are more concerned about those common issues and concerns that affect them as a religious minority; therefore, their voting behaviour is contingent upon the adequate packaging of Muslim issues. This expectation is not completely imagined. Political parties approach Muslim individuals as well as institutions as intermediaries to create a favourable equilibrium. The presence of a few Muslim faces in almost all parties is a good example to illustrate this point.

The Muslim vote bank, thus, turns out to be a logical outcome of these three formulations. Political parties evoke the constitutional identity given to Muslims to make a few political proposals. Issues which are related to the administrative discourse, such as violence against Muslims, Muslim backwardness and reservation, find a clear political overtone, and Muslim voting eventually becomes merely an object of political bargain!

Muslim voting patterns, on the contrary, demonstrate that there is no Muslim vote bank. Muslim participation in electoral politics primarily depends on issues such as employment and education. However, political parties are not keen on recognizing this fact. The BJP wants Muslims to vote as Indians, as if these are the only two ultimate identities; the Bahujan Samaj Party is not interested in Pasmanda Muslim politics, as if the question of Muslim caste is politically relevant; left parties have not yet taken up the question of the Muslim artisan classes, as if Muslims need to vote for them only for the sake of secularism; and the Congress and the Samajwadi Party are misreading the question of OBC reservation, as if reservation is given on religious lines!

The notion of the Muslim vote bank, it seems, will continue to survive, until and unless Muslim plurality is recognized as a political reality. However, its effective functioning depends on another crucial metaphor of Muslim politics—good Muslims versus bad Muslims.

Who are the good Muslims?

Elaborating on the title of his autobiography, *Sarkari Musalman*, retired Lt General Zameer Uddin Shah, the former VC of Aligarh Muslim University, argues:

> Sarkari Muslaman [. . .] meaning those who worked for the government [. . .] I faced this phrase [. . .] when I was a young Second Lieutenant. I saw a few excellent riders from Aligarh Muslim University playing Polo [. . .] I went to them and asked, 'Please join the army. We need good riders. You will also get to play polo.' As they were leaving, I asked them again, 'Will you

join the army? This is the last bastion of secularism. You will never be discriminated for being a Muslim.' No answer came from them but one of them said, 'You are a Sarkari Musalman, so you will say that.'[16]

General Shah's explanation makes us aware of the fact that the Sarkari Musalman should not be seen merely as the provocative title of a book. It is an explanatory template by which the attitudes, responses and actions of Indian Muslims, especially those who have become part of the so-called mainstream society of the nation, are described and evaluated.

This term is also used to make a distinction between favourable/acceptable Muslims and non-acceptable Muslims— the latter being the bad guys of the community.

Good Muslims, we are told, would join the mainstream, while bad Muslims would continue to raise sectarian demands and disrupt the progress of the nation. A number of different phrases are used interchangeably to describe good Muslims—secular Muslims, cultural Muslims, nationalist Muslims, and so on, to counter the bad guys—communal Muslims, separatist Muslims, pro-Pakistan elements and, more recently, terrorist Muslims.

In this sense, the Sarkari Musalman refers to an acceptable and trustworthy agent of the state/government.

The story of good Muslims versus bad Muslims is inextricably linked to the debates on postcolonial Muslim identity. It is worth noting that Hindu right wing groups—the Hindu Mahasabha as well as the BJS—did not show any interest in evoking the good versus bad Muslim binary in the 1950s. They treated all Muslims as a homogeneous entity and asked them to Indianize their identity and religion and demonstrate their loyalty and patriotism.

It was Nehru who introduced this distinction to legitimize his policies towards minorities and oppose Hindu communal politics. In a letter to Ravishankar Shukla in 1954, Nehru wrote:

There are all kinds of trends among the Muslims in India and some of them are undoubtedly objectionable. I think, however, that we should not be led away by these and we should try to judge the broad situation objectively.[17]

The more elaborated conceptualization of 'good Muslims' may be found in his letter to chief ministers in 1961. He said:

Recently, there was a Muslim convention in Delhi [. . .] My own reaction to this [. . .] was against it. Later, I came to the conclusion that it would not be right to try to stop it [. . .] I do not regret that it was held, even though I dislike much that happened there. The resolutions were not so bad, but the tenor of the speeches made was definitely bad. But, good or bad, it represented widespread feeling, and we have to recognize that and try to get rid of it. It is that feeling of frustration which leads to narrow-mindedness and reactionary thinking.[18]

Being a serious political observer, Nehru emphasized more on the reasons, which forced a section of Muslims to feel isolated after the Partition, especially in north India. But the vocabulary of 'good' and 'bad' contributed significantly to set out nationalist expectations.

After Nehru's death, a new imagination of 'good Muslims' began to take shape. More broadly, three categories of good Muslims may be underlined.

English-educated, middle-class professionals, who have/had some association with left-liberal politics, are the first type of Muslims, recognized as ideal community leaders. It is argued that this section would infuse a progressive impulse in the community and Muslims would be able to join the mainstream in the national strata. Author Khwaja Ahmad Abbas and diplomat Muhammad Yunus, are examples of this type.

The second are the favourable ulema and religious elite, who are also treated as good Muslims. Although this tradition began with Maulana Abul Kalam Azad, the manner in which controversial leaders, such as the imam of the Jama Masjid, Abdullah Bukhari, were promoted is quite astonishing. Indira Gandhi's letter to Bukahri, which she wrote in 1979, is an example of this form of politics. She wrote:

> Some incidents, including the 1975 Jama Masjid incident, which took place in the past and during the Emergency, resulted in stress and strain, and I am sorry that they left an atmosphere of misunderstanding and bitterness. Let this past be forgotten so that we can begin on a note of harmony and cooperation [. . .] We agree that all derogatory references to religious leaders should be deleted from textbooks. Our party is committed not to interfere in Muslim personal law [. . .] Urdu would be recognized as a second language to be used for official purpose in some areas.[19]

The outcome of this letter was quite obvious. The imam did not only support Indira Gandhi in the 1980 elections but also legitimized his controversial fatwa politics, which we discussed in the previous section.[20]

The rise of the BJP in recent years has led to the third category of good Muslims—nationalist (Rashtravadi) Muslims. Unlike the progressive Muslims of the Congress/left, these Muslims offer uncritical support to the basic premises of the Hindutva project. They take a pro-BJP position on controversial issues by emphasizing their religious identity as Muslims.

This is what Zafar Islam, a new Muslim face in the BJP and a staunch supporter of Prime Minister Modi, says:

> Who is keeping the Muslims out of power? It's the Muslim community which is responsible for making its votes valueless

and redundant by becoming a captive vote bank for the Congress and a few other parties, but completely ignoring the BJP which is a ruling party and works in a non-partisan manner.[21]

Faith in the scientific temperament of ancient Indian/Hindu philosophy is another quality of good Rashtravadi Muslims. The celebrated ideal of A.P.J. Abdul Kalam (a veena player, a Gita reader, a Sanskrit lover, and yet a Muslim scientist!) is a good example. This may be the reason why he was preferred over Aurangzeb—the bad Muslim—for commemorating ideal Muslimness in contemporary India.

This version of good Muslims—either as Sarkari Muslims or as nationalist ones—signifies a very specific norm of Indian politics. All political parties need Muslims for electoral survival— not merely to address, at least symbolically, the highly diversified Muslim community as voters but also to assert political influence over other social constituencies.

Good Muslims, in this framework, are shown as 'lived examples' who can fulfil the standard expectations set out for all Muslims. Thus, when Mohan Bhagwat says that Hindutva without Muslims is meaningless, he does not entirely aim at reaching out to Muslims. Instead, he is addressing common Hindus who still do not approve of Hindutva's anti-Muslim rhetoric.[22]

The 'good Muslims' of the BJP/RSS—such as Zafar Islam and Zafar Sareshwala—seem to rectify this message silently through their symbolic presence in the party.

So what are the criteria for being a good Muslim in India? This discussion illustrates three aspects of good Muslims:

1. **Cultural capital**: As part of the elite—religious and/or modern—he/she should have cultural capital (lineage, education, political–economic background) that may be used to demonstrate his/her status as a Muslim leader/representative.

His/her access to political power is an additional qualification in this regard.

2. **Acceptability:** He/she should be able to satisfy the ideal expectations set out for all Muslims.

3. **Political correctness:** He/she should always adhere to a politically correct line.

Muslim appeasement

Muslim appeasement is the third metaphor of Muslim politics. Although the term originated in colonial India—especially to describe Congress's attitude toward the Muslim League in the 1940s—it survives as a metaphor in post-1947 politics with very specific political connotations.

Broadly speaking, Muslim appeasement refers to at least two aspects of politics with regard to Muslims: biased institutional apparatus and unfair political practices.

The constitutional provisions related to the rights of religious minorities, which offer legal protection to autonomous bodies, such as Islamic endowments known as waqf, Muslim personal law and educational institutions, such as Aligarh Muslim University, are seen as problematic and unfair. It is asserted that that minority rights given in the Constitution go against the spirit of religious equality and secularism based on rule of law. An article titled 'Minorities Problems and Its Solution', written by Balraj Madhok, one of RSS's well-known intellectuals, outlines the relevant problematic aspects of the Constitution. He says:

Articles 21, 30 and 370, which are discriminatory, being in favour of minorities, should be abrogated from the Constitution of India. Such provisions [should] be made in the Constitution that no discrimination between the citizens of India will be made by the Government on the basis of religions or methods of worship [. . .]

Article 44 of the Constitution should at once be implemented for the purpose. Such provisions contained in the Muslim personal law which go against the Constitution of India and humanity [should] be declared illegal, unlawful and unconstitutional [. . .] Such Muslims and other minorities who are not prepared to abjure their separatist tendencies should be declared foreigners, and they should be divested of the right of franchise.[23]

Muslim appeasement is also used to denote specific forms of political practices. The assurance given to Muslims by political parties with regard to educational and/or economic empowerment, the distribution of tickets to Muslim candidates in elections for legislative bodies and even declaration of holidays for Muslim religious festivals are treated as Muslim appeasement. A resolution passed by the RSS in 2005 is an example of this critique:

The Akhil Bharatiya Karyakari Mandal (ABKM) decries the return of the demon of minority appeasement under the present UPA government. Its earlier decision to provide 50 per cent reservation for Muslims in Aligarh Muslim University and its attempts now to go in appeal against the HC order on the minority status of Aligarh Muslim University is a standing proof of its appeasement policy [. . .] Also reprehensible is the reported directive given to all the chief ministers of the Congress-ruled states to emulate [the] Andhra Pradesh government in extending reservations to Muslims.[24]

This Hindutva imagination of Muslim appeasement is also based on the notion of Muslim homogeneity, which we have discussed in the previous chapters of this book. All Muslims of India are envisaged as beneficiaries of minority rights and policies of the so-called secular parties. As a result, we are told, a feeling of separatism among them strengthened.

Interestingly, the secular critique of Hindutva's imagination of Muslim appeasement does not propose any alternative conceptualization. Although it tends to talk about the multilayered structure of the Muslim community and its relative marginalization, the possibilities of appeasement, its meanings, forms and impacts are not given any serious intellectual/political attention. Muslim appeasement is simply refuted as Hindutva propaganda. Even those scholars who are critical of Hindu as well as Muslim communalism could not produce any significant analysis of Muslim appeasement.

Mushirul Hasan's assessment of the Shah Bano moment in Indian politics is a good example to underline this confusion. He writes:

> Debates on the Uniform Civil Code have gone on ceaselessly since Independence. Muslim orthodoxy was unequivocally opposed to change, and the liberal view became increasingly blurred because of the unhappy intervention of Hindu ideologues as vocal proponents of reform in Muslim personal law [. . .] The government dare not change its strategy for fear of losing Muslim votes [. . .] Rajiv Gandhi imposed a ban on Salman Rushdie's book, *The Satanic Verses*, and his successor V.P. Singh declared Prophet Mohammad's birthday a national holiday. Finally, *Muslims were willfully appeased* by the Muslim Women (Protection of Rights on Divorce) Act, 1986, and through official reluctance to enact a Uniform Civil Code.[25]

It is certainly clear from this passage that Hasan is condemning Hindutva politics, which appropriated the UCC debate. He is equally critical of Islamic orthodoxy, which was supported by the state in the Shah Bano case. Yet, Hasan fails to specify his reading of 'Muslim appeasement' and we are left with a few puzzling questions: Does Muslim appeasement only mean the political moves of the Rajiv Gandhi government? Or does it mean that all Muslims were going to vote for Rajiv Gandhi in the election because they were 'wilfully appeased' in the Shah Bano case? If this is the case, how is Hasan's notion of Muslim appeasement different from the RSS's conceptualization?

The publication of the Sachar report gave a new twist to the idea of Muslim appeasement. As an official document, the report underlines the fact that the Muslims of India are socially, economically and educationally backward and marginalized. Although the report very categorically emphasizes upon the highly diverse and deeply stratified structure of the Muslim community, 'Muslim victimhood' as a new template of Indian politics began to take shape. The report was invoked, particularly by non-BJP parties, to demonstrate that Muslim appeasement was a myth created by Hindutva forces and that Muslims must be treated as an excluded community.

Interestingly, Hindutva politics also refashioned itself in the light of this response. It was argued that the Congress did not show any serious interest in the empowerment of Muslims; they were treated as a vote bank, which led to their marginalization and exclusion. The BJP's firm commitment to equal treatment to all, as the argument goes, helped even Muslims to prosper in the BJP-ruled states. L.K. Advani's assessment of the Sachar report may be cited here. He said:

> Generally speaking, by now, people have widely come to acknowledge that in terms of honest governance and development of Gujarat, Narendra Bhai's achievements are beyond dispute. What is often questioned is how harmonious are inter-communal relations in the state, and specifically speaking, how happy and contented the Muslims are in the State [. . .]

In setting up the Sachar Committee, [the] government had its own objectives. But going through the comparative statistics compiled by the committee, I feel Gujarat should be grateful to Justice Sachar for proving convincingly to the country that under Narendra Bhai Modi's regime, Muslims are far better off than their compatriots in other states.[26]

This argument later evolved in party rhetoric—*development of all, appeasement of none*!

Muslim appeasement has found new political life in post 2014-India. The BJP has successfully established the fact that addressing Muslims as Muslims is an act of appeasement. The impact of this assertion is so powerful that even so-called secular, anti-Hindutva and non-BJP parties have gradually started distancing themselves from Muslims, simply to avoid the tag of Muslim appeasement. This development goes against the narrative of Muslim victimhood, which dominated public discourse in the 2000s.

Let us conclude this discussion by underlining three broad three observations:

1. Muslim appeasement is not a description of an objective, sociopolitical condition of Muslims. Rather, it is a metaphor of politics, which is used primarily to criticize the policies and politics related to Muslims.

2. Although Muslim appeasement relies on Muslim homogeneity, an undifferentiated picture of a single Muslim community, recognized 'good Muslims' are never treated as beneficiaries of appeasement. In fact, good Muslims of different political parties struggle with each other as organic intellectuals either to refute Muslim appeasement as a myth or to evoke the 'Development of All, Appeasement of None' slogan.

3. The presence of these good Muslims in political parties underlines the fact that Muslim appeasement is an unwritten norm of Indian politics. A section of Muslims is always given priority over others by all political parties in order to promote a socially inclusive image. Muslim elites are given key positions to create political equilibrium. The Modi-led BJP is not an exception in this regard. The Muslim faces of the BJP, such as Mukhtar Abbas Naqvi, Zafar Islam and Najma Heptulla, are elite Muslims, who are now being appeased in the name of 'Sabka Saath, Sabka Vikas'!

10

Muslims and the Future of India's Democracy

Finding Siyasi Muslims: The three main arguments

Prime Minister Atal Bihari Vajpayee, 2002:

> Wherever Muslims live, they don't like to live in co-existence with others, they don't like to mingle with others; and instead of propagating their ideas in a peaceful manner, they want to spread their faith by resorting to terror and threats. The world has become alert to this danger.[1]

Prime Minister Manmohan Singh, 2005:

> I take pride in the fact that, although we have 150 million Muslims in our country as citizens, not one has been found to have joined the ranks of Al Qaeda or participated in the activities of the Taliban [. . .] this is because India is a functioning democracy. We are a secular state where all sections of the communities, regardless of religion, caste and creed, they may belong to [. . .] [are part of a] a democracy, being a secular democracy where all religions are free to practise their respective faiths

without fear, without favour. I think that's something which has prevented that sort of eventuality.[2]

Prime Minister Narendra Modi, 2016:

Fifty years ago, Pandit Upadhyaya said, 'Do not reward/appease (*puraskrit*) Muslims, do not shun (*tiraskrit*) them but purify (*parishkar*) them.' Do not treat Muslims like *vote ki mandi ka maal* (vote banks) or *ghrina ki vastu* (object of hatred). *Unhe apna samjho* (regard them as your own).[3]

These three Muslim images—a radical Muslim image of a jihadi community which cannot live with others peacefully, a secular Muslim image of a peace-loving nationalist community which opposes jihadi Islam and an alienated Muslim community, reluctant to take part in the national mainstream—dominate our public discourse in an interesting manner. These conflicting versions of Muslimness are often pitted against each other as conclusive factual statements. Public intellectuals, political observers and commentators, the religious–political elite and even political parties confidently take positions on Muslim issues as if there is no need to know about them. No one bothers to recognize the fact that around 14 per cent of Indians identify themselves as Muslims. Making any decisive statement about such a large number of people, who are inevitably diversified and different from each other in a number of ways, is highly misleading and inappropriate.

This book has made a modest attempt to move away from this dominant mode of thinking about Muslims. Instead of supporting or opposing any given political position on Muslims, I have tried to examine a few sociocultural sources, which produce different imaginations of the Muslim political identity in contemporary India. That is the reason why the term 'siyasi Muslims' is invoked.

The book responds to the two basic questions it poses in the Introduction: the sources of Muslim political identity and the possibilities of imagining Muslims as a political community.

The story of the colonial census, which is discussed in the first chapter, tells us that introduction of modern enumeration practices in India—drawing up a head count on the basis of religion—produced the idea of a pan-Islamic Muslim community. The debate on political representation in colonial India sustained this imagination of Muslim homogeneity and, as a result, the concept of Hindus as a permanent majority and Muslims as a permanent minority emerged.

The Indian Constitution remains critical to the idea of a permanent minority. This constitutional mandate led to the realization that there should be a clear distinction between contextually constituted political minorities and the fixed census categories such as Hindu, Muslim, Sikh, etc. Two constitutional principles—(a) Minorities should always be defined on a contextual basis and (b) The criterion for the identification of a minority should remain open and ever evolving—were set out in this regard.

However, this positive refashioning of constitutional principles found a very different overtone in the realm of competitive electoral politics. Although political parties began addressing the voters as minority and majority, the actual expressions were never delinked from the established colonial idioms of politics: Muslims as minority and Hindus as majority. The evolution of certain institutions, such as the Minorities Commission and the National Commission for Minorities, further contributed to this grand imagination of Muslim political identity. Muslim homogeneity, in fact, received official recognition in 1993, when Muslims were defined as a recognizable 'national minority'.

This brings us to the first argument of this book.

I argue that characterizing Muslims as a 'political community' is a post-1947 political formulation, which revolves around three metaphors of Muslim politics—Muslim vote bank, good Muslims/bad Muslims and Muslim appeasement. These metaphors legitimize and sustain Muslim homogeneity and restrict the possibility of any serious discussion on diversified Muslim political behaviour.

To respond to this oversimplified representation of Muslim identity, the second part of the book examines three crucial sociological dimensions—caste, gender and class. We find that sociological plurality among Muslims determines the nature of internal Muslim debates. For instance, Muslim backwardness is not a settled issue. A section of Muslims argue that all Muslims must be treated as a backward community on the basis of social and educational backwardness. On the other hand, the Pasmanda groups do not subscribe to this position. They want a rational secularization of affirmative action so that Muslim Dalits could be included in the SC category.

Internal debates on the triple talaq issue also reflect this Muslim diversity of opinion. Issues raised by the BMMA and other Muslim women organizations, such as the economic empowerment of women and having an egalitarian and gender-just Islamic family law in India, simply go against the Islamist Muslim men versus radical, anti-Islamic Muslim women binary. Interestingly, however, the government did not pay attention to such distinctive arguments and continued to recognize the ulema class represented by the AIMPLB as its main adversary. The rise of a new Muslim middle class and its progression into the Muslim elite is another powerful example that reflects the socio-economic stratification among Muslims. This class recognizes its vested interest and moves freely in the sphere of politics.

This takes us to our second argument.

Contemporary Islamic religiosities as well as the given narrative of Muslim victimhood are inextricably linked to the internal configuration of power among Muslims in India.

The book has paid close attention to the anti-Muslim rhetoric of Hindutva and its violent manifestations. We find that Muslim homogeneity not only helps Hindutva construct an ideal 'other' but also contributes in defining the contours of a particular kind of political imagination of India as a nation. This Muslim otherness is also used by the Muslim elite as well as the so-called secular parties to legitimize their political existence.

The recognition of this mutual dependence is my third argument.

I argue that Hindutva needs Muslims, and precisely for this reason the Muslim elite/non-Hindutva forces also need Hindutva to create and sustain a fear psyche among Muslims.

Will these arguments be useful in making sense of the outcome of the 2019 elections, and will they sustain beyond that? I would like to clarify that the findings of this research are based on a context-driven analysis. Therefore, the purpose of the arguments is to explain the here and now, not to predict what ought to be the future of politics! However, the explanatory capability of a context-based argument may be used to make a few broad observations, especially about Muslim political behaviour. For this purpose, I would like to deal with an important yet unexplained issue: the political silence of Muslims in contemporary India!

Silent yet siyasi Muslims

Why don't Indian Muslims react to aggressive Hindutva politics? Are they really terrified? Or is there any strategy behind this extraordinary calmness? These questions are not asked directly; yet, they do exist in our public debates as unspoken anxieties. Rejuvenated post-2014 Hindutva politics reworked on its anti-Muslim project and transformed every aspect of the social and cultural life of Muslims in India into an unsolvable contestation.

In the past four years, we have been repeatedly told that Muslims' eating habits are anti-Hindu/anti-national as they eat beef; that Muslim men don't love, they do love-jihad with Hindu girls; that Muslim couples deliberately have sex to increase their community's population so as to outnumber the Hindus; and that they offer namaz on roads to convert public (read Hindu) lands into mosque territory! This propaganda is followed by actual violence against Muslims—lynching, molestation and even rape.

Despite this hostile anti-Muslim attitude, Muslim communities do not get involved in any anti-Hindutva counter mobilization. Muslim religious organizations and pressure groups and even Muslim political leaders (except a few unknown faces who appear on prime-time TV every night!) do not argue for any Muslim mass protest. It is, therefore, possible to infer that Muslims have decided to remain silent to avoid any confrontation with Hindutva and that they would open their card in 2019.

This simple conclusion is problematic. The anxiety called 'Muslim silence' must be unravelled for a deeper analysis based on some concrete evidence. Two counter questions may be asked: (a) Has Muslim political attitude changed, especially with regard to identity-related Muslim issues? (b) Do Muslims think differently from other communities in India?

It is worth noting that the BJP has been using Muslim identity as an 'other' to cultivate its Hindutva vote bank. Post-2014 BJP politics marks a decisive shift in this regard. Unlike the previous NDA government, the Modi-led BJP decided to deliberately demolish Muslim issues in a more direct fashion. Obviously, any radical Muslim reaction would have given the government an opportunity to promote its political image as a truly nationalist establishment.

However, Muslim reactions were very different. We have seen in Chapter 7 that the triple talaq issue could not create a Shah Bano–type hype, primarily because there was strong social opposition to this practice among Hanafi Muslims, especially in north India. Even the AIMPLB failed to mobilize Muslim public opinion in its favour.

Similarly, the abolition of the Hajj subsidy remained a non-issue, as there has always been a consensus that Hajj travel should be liberalized. Violent cow politics also failed, as eating cow-meat is a highly insignificant matter for Muslim communities in India. That might be the reason why lynching as a preferred mode of violence against individual Muslims has increased in order to keep cow politics alive.

To understand this complex Muslim reaction, we must take the Babri Masjid issue as a relevant example. The CSDS-Lokniti surveys have shown that, over the years, Muslim opinion about the Babri mosque has changed quite considerably. For instance, in 2009, around 80 per cent of Muslims argued that the demolition of the mosque was an unjustified act. This feeling of injustice seems to increase in 2015, when 86 per cent Muslims all over India argued that the demise of the Babri Masjid cannot be justified at all (see Table 1 below).

Table 1: Was the demolition of the Babri Masjid justified?

	2009*			2015**		
	Justified	Unjustified	Don't know	Justified	Unjustified	Don't know
Hindu	26	48	26	33	32	35
Muslim	5	80	15	4	86	10

Source: *NES 2009, CSDS-Lokniti Data Unit; **Religious Attitude Survey 2015, CSDS-Lokniti Data Unit
Note: Figures in percentages

Question asked: Some people say that the demolition was justified while others say it was not justified. What would you say—was it justified or not?

It is not that this 'historic injustice' could only be rectified by building the Babri Masjid again. In fact, one encounters much diversified Muslim opinion on this question. In 2009, 44 per cent of Muslims claimed that only the mosque should be built on that site, while 25 per cent suggested that a Ram temple along with the Babri Masjid might be constructed side by side to solve this issue. Muslim opinion in favour of 'mosque with temple' consolidated in 2015 as the most appropriate solution for the dispute (see Table 2 on the following page).

In fact, this may be the reason why a majority of Muslims feel that the issue must be solved through the court of law, though the possibility of a negotiated settlement outside court is also seen as a strong possibility (see Table 3 on p. 197).

Does it mean that the Babri Masjid still survives as an important Muslim issue? In the 2016 UP Assembly elections, 32 per cent of Muslims argued that the Babri Masjid issue was not important for them, while one-fourth of the respondents decided not to answer this question! (See Table 4 on p. 197.) It simply means that although Muslims feel that the demolition of the mosque was a highly unjust issue, they do not have any serious interest in it. After all, the mosque has long been demolished to create a functional temple in Ayodhya! In other words, the Babri Masjid, like other identity-centric Muslim issues, has lost its capacity to be a cause of provocation for Muslims.

Table 2: What should be the solution for the Babri Masjid–Ram temple dispute?

	2009*					2015**				
	Neither mosque nor temple	Mosque should be built	Temple should be built	Both mosque and temple	Others	No opinion	Neither mosque nor temple	Mosque should be built	Temple should be built	Both mosque and temple	Others	No opinion
Hindu	15	7	25	25	4	25	7	2	33	29	2	27
Muslim	11	44	1	25	3	16	8	35	1	34	3	19

Source: *NES 2009 CSDS-Lokniti Data Unit;
**Religious Attitude Survey 2015, CSDS-Lokniti Data Unit
Note: Figures in percentages

Table 3: How should the mosque–temple issue be solved?

	Supreme Court	Discussion outside Court	Law by Parliament	Others	No response
Hindu	43	25	9	2	19
Muslim	40	21	8	4	25

Source: Mood of the Nation Survey 2017, CSDS-Lokniti Data Unit
Note: Figures in percentages

Question asked: People have different opinions about how the temple–mosque issue of Ayodhya should be resolved. Some say it should be resolved by the Supreme Court. What's your opinion?

Table 4: Does the Babri Masjid matter?

	Very important	Somewhat important	Not very important	Not at all important	No answer
Hindu	19	21	16	19	23
Muslim	24	16	16	16	25

Source: UP Assembly Election Survey 2017; CSDS-Lokniti Data Unit
Note: Figures in percentages

Question: How important is the Ram Mandir–Babri Masjid issue going to be for you in the forthcoming Assembly elections? Very important, somewhat important, not very important or not at all important?

To understand the visible calmness of Muslims in contemporary India, we must also have a look at Muslim opinion in relation to what is called national sentiment.

The CSDS-Lokniti's recent Mood of the Nation survey offers us another set of important findings. The survey finds that the popularity of the BJP-led NDA government is declining. Muslim respondents also share this view. They strongly believe that the Modi government should not be given another chance. This Muslim opposition to the present regime, we must note, does not deviate from the national sentiment as a majority of the respondents (47 per cent) argue that the Modi government is not good for the country.

Similarly, the Muslim response to the present state of affairs is not very different from that of other communities. Muslims seem to assert, more stridently, in fact, that India as a country requires a better government that could provide a positive direction to the nation (see Table 6 on the following page).

The Muslim assertion against the Modi government is also linked to the evolving environment of hate against all marginalized groups in the country. Table 7 on p. 200 shows that a majority of Indians feel that atrocities committed against the weaker sections of the society are not dealt with adequately by the government. They seem to suggest that the state does not demonstrate a clear attitude against those who create an atmosphere of hate and terror. This is also true about the violence against Muslims. More than half of the respondents asserted that they are not satisfied with the way in which miscreants, such as the gau rakshaks (protectors of cows), are dealt with by the government.

These figures also underline the fact that the Muslims of India do share the national view on a few fundamental issues that India faces as a national community of citizens. At the same time, being the main target of Hindutva politics, Muslims appear to be more concerned and dissatisfied with the present regime. By this logic, the Muslim silence is nothing but a reflection of political indifference, which has emerged as a norm of non-Hindutva politics in the last few years.

Table 5: Does the Modi government deserve a second chance?

	Yes	No	No response
Overall	39	47	14
Hindus	44	42	14
Muslims	15	75	10
Sikhs	31	56	13
Christians	17	62	21

Source: MOTN Survey, May 2018; CSDS-Lokniti Data Unit
Note: Figures in percentages

Table 6: Are we going in the right direction as a country?

	Yes	No	No response
Overall	35	44	21
Hindus	38	41	21
Muslims	18	63	19
Sikhs	27	58	15
Christians	20	61	19

Source: MOTN Survey, May 2018; CSDS-Lokniti Data Unit
Note: Figures in percentages

Question asked: In general, do you think things in the country are headed in the right direction or the wrong direction?

Table 7: National sentiment and the violence against marginalized groups

	Satisfied with the attitude shown by the govt.	Dissatisfied with the attitude shown by the govt.	No response
Atrocities against Dalits (responses of all respondents)	40	49	11
Atrocities against Dalits (Dalit respondents only)	30	60	10
Atrocities against Adivasis (responses of all respondents)	36	50	11
Atrocities against Adivasis (Adivasi Respondents only)	33	54	13
Violence against Muslims (responses of all respondents)	34	53	13
Violence against Muslims (Muslim respondents only)	16	79	5
Crimes against women/girls (responses of all respondents)	31	61	8

	Satisfied with the attitude shown by the govt.	Dissatisfied with the attitude shown by the govt.	No response
Crimes against women/ girls (female respondents only)	29	60	11

Source: MOTN Survey, May 2018; CSDS-Lokniti Data Unit
Note: Fully and somewhat 'satisfied' or 'dissatisfied' categories have been merged as 'satisfied' and 'dissatisfied' in this table. Figures in percentages

Question asked: Are you satisfied or dissatisfied with the attitude/ concern shown by the Modi government towards the following incidents?

The possibilities of any 'Muslim reaction' must also be seen in relation to the demographic plurality of Indian Muslims, which we have discussed in previous chapters of the book. As I argue that the Muslim community consists of a number of diversified Islamic communities, which speak different languages, live in different regions of the country, and even follow varied versions of Islam as a religion. In the backdrop of this apparent heterogeneity, the idea of having a defined strategy to counter Hindutva seems unreasonable and vague.

Muslim silence, on the other hand, points towards the intellectual weakness of the political class. Contemporary BJP Hindutva has failed to produce any constructive and positive programme of action for Muslims as a 'community of communities'. Hindutva survives because of its reactionary position on Islam and Muslims. Non-BJP parties have also failed to articulate any new perspective on Muslims in the absence of old identity-based issues, in which Muslims do not have any interest.

To conclude, I make a futurist observation. The political class must realize that Muslim aspirations cannot be reduced to so-called Muslim issues alone. Muslims, like other socio-religious communities, are more concerned about poverty, employment and education. No doubt, the threat to religious identity affects them psychologically, but the commonly given imaginations of siyasi Muslims do not entirely determine their aspirations as citizens.

Notes

Introduction: Muslims as a Political Question

1. Radhika Ramaseshan, 'Modi chants purification mantra', *Telegraph*, 26 September 2016, https://bit.ly/2WoU0Dy.
2. Varghese K. George and Gargi Parsai, 'Exclusive interview with Amit Shah', *The Hindu*, 2 February 2015, https://bit.ly/2CypsGb.
3. 'BJP president Amit Shah charged in Muzaffarnagar hate speech case', *Times of India*, 10 September 2014, https://bit.ly/2RoAZ0a.
4. Syed Zafar Islam, 'Why Muslims must give BJP a fair chance', *Indian Express*, 4 May 2017, https://bit.ly/2HDr2w8.
5. Ibid.
6. 'Muslim Man in Hisar Assaulted For Not Saying "Vande Mataram"; One Arrested', Wire, 13 July 2017, https://bit.ly/2Uom3kB.

PART I: MAKING SENSE OF SIYASI MUSLIMS

Chapter 1: Muslims, We Know as 'Numbers'!

1. Ramachandra Guha, 'Liberals, sadly', *Indian Express*, 24 March 2018, https://bit.ly/2DDfNzM.
2. Ramachandra Guha, 'Burdens of the past', *Indian Express*, 10 April 2018, https://bit.ly/2CQNLiQ.
3. Ibid.

4. Sagnik Chowdhury, Abantika Ghosh and Ruhi Tewari, 'Census 2011: Hindus dip to below 80 per cent of population; Muslim share up, slows down', *Indian Express*, 27 August 1015, https://bit.ly/2UqGjCf.

5. Gyan Varma, Anuja, Pretika Khanna, 'Census 2011 shows Islam is the fastest growing religion in India', LiveMint, 26 August 2015, https://bit.ly/2RRMTF5.

6. Saibal Sen, 'Bengal beats India in Muslim growth rate', *Times of India*, 26 August 2015, https://bit.ly/2Tn7kXa.

7. Mehar Singh Gill, 'Politics of Population Census Data in India', *Economic and Political Weekly* 42, no. 3 (20–26 January 2007): pp. 241–49.

8. Jeffery Roger and Jeffery Patricia, 'Saffron Demography, Common Wisdom, Aspirations and Uneven Governmentalities', *Economic and Political Weekly* 40, no. 5 (2005): pp. 447–53.

9. Ashutosh Bhardwaj, 'Review policy to check Muslim, Christian population: RSS resolution', *Indian Express*, 1 November 2015, https://bit.ly/2CSpOaI.

10. Abusaleh Shariff, 'Myth of Muslim growth', *Indian Express*, 2 September 2015, https://bit.ly/2COo4Q0.

11. Jeffery Roger and Jeffery Patricia, 'Saffron Demography'.

12. John Strachey, *India* (London: Kegan Paul, Trench, Turner & Co. Ltd, 1894), pp. 3–5.

13. Ibid., p. 235.

14. Id.

15. Id., p. 240.

16. Id., p. 241.

17. *General Report on the Census of India, 1891* (London: Her Majesty's Stationery Office, 1893), p. 174.

18. Ibid., p. 175.

19. James Mill, *The History of British India*, vol. 3 (London: Baldwin, Cradock, and Joy, 1826), p. 207.

20. Ibid., p. 430.

21. Id., p. 457.

22. Partha Chatterjee, *The Nations and Its Fragments: Colonial and Postcolonial Histories* (New Delhi: Oxford University Press, 1993) pp. 19–32.

23. Reginald Coupland, *The Indian Problem: Report on the Constitutional Problem in India* (London and New York: Oxford University Press, 1944), pp. 34–35.

24. Ibid., p. 36.
25. Id.
26. *Report of the Indian Franchise Committee*, vol. 1. (Calcutta: Central Publication Branch, 1932), pp. 175–78.
27. A.G. Noorani, ed, *The Muslims of India: A Documentary Record* (New Delhi: Oxford University Press, 2003), pp. 63–64.
28. Ibid., p. 57.
29. Maulana Abul Kalam, *India Wins Freedom* (New Delhi: Orient Longman, 1988), pp. 247–48.
30. B.R. Ambedkar, *Pakistan or the Partition of India* (Bombay: Thacker & Co. Ltd, 1943), https://bit.ly/22jzqPO.
31. Ibid.

Chapter 2: Muslims as a Religious Community

1. Jignesh Patel, 'Truth Behind Boy Tearing India Flag, Saying "Pakka Musalman Hoon"', Quint, 22 August 2018, https://bit.ly/2DJOPXb.
2. Suresh Chavhanke, Twitter post, 20 August 2018, https://bit.ly/2WsPuUq.
3. Jignesh Patel, 'Truth Behind Boy Tearing India Flag'.
4. Syeda Saiyidain Hameed, ed and trans., *Hali's Musaddas: A Story in Verse of the Ebb and Tide of Islam* (New Delhi: HarperCollins, 2003), pp. 170–71.

Chapter 3: 'Islamization' since Independence!

1. Mohammed A. Kalam, 'Religious conversions in Tamil Nadu: can these be viewed as protest movements', *Indian Anthropologist* 20, no. 1/2 (1990): pp. 39–48.
2. RSS Resolution: ABKM 1981: Meenakshipuram Conversion.
3. Shaikh, Farzana, *Community and Consensus in Islam: Muslim Representation in Colonial India, 1860–1947* (Cambridge: Cambridge University Press, 1991), pp. 49–53.
4. Ziya-ul-Hasan Faruqi, *The Deoband School and the Demand for Pakistan* (Calcutta: Asia Publishing House, 1963), pp. 113–19.
5. 5. Barbara D. Metcalf, *Husain Ahmad Madani: The Jihad for Islam and India's Freedom* (Oxford: Oneworld Publications, 2008); and Muhammad Qasim Zaman, *The Ulama in Contemporary Islam*:

Custodians of Change (Princeton and Oxford: Princeton University Press, 2007).

6. Christian W. Troll, 'Two Conceptions of Da'wá in India: Jamā'at-i Islāmi and Tablīghī Jamā'at', *Archives de sciences sociales des religions*, 39e Année, No. 87 (1994): pp. 115–33.

7. Abul Ala Maududi, *A Historic Address at Madras*, trans. Mohammad Siddiqui Naveed (New Delhi: Markazi Maktaba Islami Publishers, 2009), p. 32.

8. Ibid., p. 32.

9. I focus on the works of Maulana Yusuf as he led the Tablighi Jamaat in the crucial years in the post-Partition period, especially in the 1960s, when a new phase of Muslim politics began. *See*, Hilal Ahmed, *Muslim Political Discourse in Postcolonial India: Monuments, Memory, Contestation* (London and New Delhi: Routledge, 2014).

10. Mufti Mohammad Roshan Shah Qasmi, *Malfoozat wa Iqtebasaat Maulana Mohammad Yusuf Kandhlawi* (New Delhi: Rashid Publications, N.D.), p. 19.

11. Ibid., p. 20.

12. Barbara D. Metcalf, 'Living Hadith in the Tablīghī Jama'āt', *Journal of Asian Studies* 52, no. 03 (1993): pp. 603–05.

13. Mufti Mohammad Roshan Shah Qasmi, *Malfoozat wa Iqtebasaat Maulana Mohammad Yusuf Kandhlawi*, p. 46.

14. For a historical evaluation of these six principles, *see* Syed Abul Hasan Ali, *Life and Mission of Maulana Mohammad Ilyas* (Lucknow: Academy of Islamic Research & Publications, 2012), pp. 40–59.

15. Yoginder Sikand, 'Arya Shuddhi and Muslim Tabligh: Muslim Reactions to Arya Samaj Proselytization (1923–30), in *Religious Conversion in India: Modes, Motivations, Meanings*, eds Rowena Robinson and Sathianathan Clarke (New Delhi: Oxford University Press, 2003), pp. 98–117.

16. Irfan Ahmad, *Islamism and Democracy in India: The Transformation of Jamaat-e-Islami* (Princeton: Princeton University Press, 2010); and Jamal Malik, *Islam in South Asia: A Short History* (New Delhi: Orient BlackSwan, 2012), pp. 403–35.

17. Abul Lais Islahi Nadwi, *Bharat ka Navnirman Aur Hum* (Rebuilding of India and Our Role), trans. Afzal Husaain (New Delhi: Markazi Maktaba Islami Publishers, 2014), pp. 31–32.

18. Abul Ala Maududi, *Pavitr Quran* (New Delhi: MMI, 1970).

19. Arshad Madani and Muhammad Sulaiman, *Quaran Sharif: Anuwad aur Vyakhya* (New Delhi: Jamiat Ulama e-Hind, 1992), pp. ii–v.

20. Jamaat-e-Islami Hind's emphasis on Hindi should be seen in this political context in which Urdu turns out to be a minority (read Muslim) language. *See* Paul Brass, *Language, Religion and Politics in North India* (Cambridge: Cambridge University Press, 1974), pp. 182–217.

21. Maulana Wahiduddin Khan, *Conversion: An Intellectual Transformation*, e-book, https://bit.ly/2SrmflQ.

22. Maulana Wahiduddin Khan, *Three Stages of Da'wah Work*, e-book, https://bit.ly/2DGJ5MM.

23. Ibid.

24. Id.

25. For an elaboration of this point, *see* Syed Abul Hasan Ali Nadwi, *Live to Lead: A Call to Indian Muslims*, trans. Shah Ebadur Rahman (Lucknow: Academy of Islamic Research & Publications, 1980), https://bit.ly/2Ga9qq5.

26. Syed Abul Hasan Ali Nadwi, *Inviting to the Way of Allah* (London: Ta-Ha Publishers Ltd and UK Islamic Academy, 1992), p. 9, https://bit.ly/2HQNZfA.

27. Ibid., p. 17.

28. Syed Abul Hasan Ali Nadwi, *Appreciation and Interpretation of Religion in the Modern Age*, trans. Syed Athar Husain (Lucknow: Academy of Islamic Research & Publications, 1980), p. 4.

29. Nadwi was one of the founder members of the All India Muslim Personal Law Board, which was established in 1972. This was the first time he was actively participating in an issue which had already taken a clear political shape. However, he emerged as the leading politically inclined religious scholar in the time following the Shah Bano case (1985). For Nadwi's changing understanding of politics, *see* Syed Abul Hasan Ali Nadwi, *Karwan-e-Zindagi* (Lucknow: Matkaba-e-Islam, 2003).

30. Ibid., pp. 154–62.

31. Syed Abul Hasan Ali Nadwi, *Muslims in India*, trans. Mohammad Asif Kidwai (Lucknow: Academy of Islamic Research & Publications, 1976), p. 3.

32. Ibid., p. 9. *See* also Jamal Malik, 'A.H. Ali Nadwi', in *Historical Thinking in South Asia: A Handbook of Sources from Colonial Times to the Present*, ed. Michael Gottlob (New Delhi: Oxford University Press, 2003), pp. 242–46.

33. Syed Abul Hasan Ali Nadwi, *Muslims in India*, p. 5.

34. This argument is elaborated in two small books penned by Nadwi in the post-1986 period. *See* Syed Abul Hasan Ali Nadwi, *Hindustani*

Musalman Ek Drishti Mein (An Overview of Indian Muslims) (New Delhi: Markazi Maktaba Islami Publishers, 2014); and Syed Abul Hasan Ali Nadwi, *Try to Understand the Problems and Sentiments of Indian Muslims: A Prerequisite for Peaceful Co-existence* (Lucknow: All India Solidarity Forum, N.D.).

35. Hilal Ahmed, 'Naik, Zakir', *Oxford Islamic Studies Online* https://bit.ly/2I2QMT9.

36. Ibid.

37. Id.

38. Id.

39. Id.

40. Emphasis added; Vidya and Sahil Joshi, 'Full text of Zakir Naik's open letter to India: Ban timed with demonetisation to escape resistance', *India Today*, 25 November 2016, https://bit.ly/2UFLGO0.

Chapter 4: Why Does Hindutva Need Muslims?

1. 'Bharat of Future: An RSS Perspective (Day 1)', Rashtriya Swayamsevak Sangh, 18 September 2018: 'हिन्दुत्व उस मूल्य समुच्चय का नाम है। विविधता में एकता, समन्वय, त्याग, संयम, कृतज्ञता। इसका आधार जो सत्य है उसका अन्वेषण हमारे यहां किया गया।'

2. Ibid.: 'सभी भारत से निकले सम्प्रदायों का जो सामूहिक मूल्य बोध है उसका नाम हिन्दुत्व है। . . . इसलिये हम जिसको हिन्दुत्व कहते हैं उस मूल्यबोध, उससे निकली हुई यह संस्कृति, उसके साथ दूसरा घटक है देशभक्ति। वो भारत की पहचान है। भारत इसके लिए है।'

3. Id.: 'हमारी चलती आई हुई विचारधारा है उसको दुनिया हिंदुत्व कहती है, इसलिये हम कहते हैं कि हमारा हिन्दू राष्ट्र है।'

4. Id.: 'हिन्दुत्व के हम तीन आधार मानते हैं। देशभक्ति, पूर्वज गौरव और संस्कृति।'

5. 'Bharat of Future: Lecture Series by Dr Mohan Bhagwat (Day 3)', Rashtriya Swayamsevak Sangh, 20 September 2018: 'इसका मतलब इसमें मुसलमान नहीं चाहिए ऐसा बिल्कुल नहीं होता। जिस दिन ये कहा जाएगा कि हां मुसलमान नहीं चाहिए उस दिन यह हिंदुत्व नहीं रहेगा।'

6. 'We do not discriminate people on the bases of sect, community, language, and caste. We simply emphasize on motherland, heritage of our forefathers and the our unique culture. These are the elements of our nationality.'

7. Kanchan Vasdev, 'Hindutva is being misunderstood, our people responsible: BJP MP Shanta Kumar', *Indian Express*, 2 November 2017, https://bit.ly/2Bl2XVp.

8. V.D. Savarkar, *Hindutva: Who is a Hindu?* (Bombay: Veer Savarkar Prakashan, 1969), pp. 115–16.

9. M.S. Golwalkar, *Bunch of Thoughts*, https://bit.ly/2Bfhh1C.
10. Rakesh Sinha, 'Of swayamsevaks and intellectuals', *Indian Express*, 24 March 2017, https://bit.ly/2t43AOw.
11. *Bunch of Thoughts*, p. 63.
12. 'Hindu Agenda', Vishva Hindu Parishad, https://bit.ly/2HRkeuX.
13. 'Vision and Mission', Vishva Hindu Parishad, 22 October 2012, https://bit.ly/2BfiBS8.
14. 'Chapter 2: Our National Identity', Bharatiya Janata Party, https://bit.ly/2RElUrk.
15. Ibid.
16. *Constitution and Rules*, Bharatiya Janata Party, September 2012, https://bit.ly/2GauRrj.
17. 'Philosophy: Integral Humanism', Bharatiya Janata Party, https://bit.ly/2TweBDV.
18. Ibid.
19. Emphasis added; 'Philosophy: Integral Humanism', BJP Gujarat, https://bit.ly/2GnhiDW.
20. *Dr Ramesh Prabhoo vs Prabhakar K. Kunte* (1996 SCC [1], AIR 1996 1113).
21. 'Politicians misusing my judgment on Hinduism: Justice Verma', Rediff.com, 5 February 2003, https://bit.ly/2UFTcs9.
22. Arkamoy Dutta Majumdar, 'Indian Muslims must realise their forefathers were Hindus: RSS chief Mohan Bhagwat', LiveMint, 3 October 2017, https://bit.ly/2S68rh2.
23. V.D. Savarkar, *Hindutva: Who is a Hindu?*, pp. 113.
24. Rakesh Sinha, *Shri Guruji and Indian Muslims*, https://bit.ly/2BjbIPA.
25. Bharatiya Jana Sangh—Party Documents, vol. 1, BJS publication, New Delhi, p. 49.
26. Ibid., p. 104.

PART II: UNPACKING THE SIYASI MUSLIM

Chapter 5: Muslims as a Minority

1. 'Muslims are not minorities, Parsis are: Najma Heptulla', *Times of India*, 28 May 2014, https://bit.ly/2SagklQ.
2. 'Muslims feeling alienated since Independence, says Minority Affairs Minister Najma Heptulla', Firstpost, 24 May 2015, https://bit.ly/2D48fVj.

3. Saurabh Gupta, 'Union Minister Najma Heptulla's Stand on Muslim Reservation Upsets Minority Community', NDTV.com, 3 January 2015, https://bit.ly/2WGqaug.

4. 'Resolution Adopted by the National Integration Conference', 1961, *see* Sachchidananda. 'Sociology of National Integration', *Bulletin of the Deccan College Research Institute* 31/32, no. 1/2 (1970–71/1971–72): pp. 193–201.

5. Tahir Mahmood, *Minorities Commission 1978–2015: Minor Role in Major Affairs* (New Delhi: LexisNexis-Universal, 2016), p. 32.

6. Ibid., p. 34

7. Id., pp. 71–72.

8. *DAV College Etc. vs State of Punjab & Ors*, 5 May 1971 (AIR 1971 1737, 1971 SCR 688).

9. Ibid.

10. *T.M.A Pai Foundation & Ors vs State of Karnataka & Ors*, 2002

11. Tahir Mahmood, *Minorities Commission 1978–2015*, pp. 129–30.

12. Ibid.

13. The Citizenship Amendment Bill 2016.

14. This proposed citizenship bill should also be seen in relation to the debate on the National Register of Citizens (NRC). Technically, the NCR is the official register containing the names of all Indian citizens. The NCR was prepared in 1951 after publication of the first postcolonial census. The NCR became very relevant in the context of Assam in the post-1986 period, when the citizenship law was amended to determine the status of migrants in the state (Roy, 2016, 45–51). The process of updating the NCR is based on the revised cut-off date. The names of those persons (or their descendants) who appear in the NRC, 1951, or in any of the official documents up to the midnight of 24 March 1971, which would prove their presence in Assam or in any part of India, are to be recognized as Indian citizens. The draft NCR was published on 30 July 2018, which has excluded around 40,000 people living in Assam.

15. *Jamia Teachers' Association vs The Vice Chancellor, Jamia Millia Islamia, & Ors*, National Commission for Minority Educational Institutions (NCMEI), Case No. 1443 of 2006, https://bit.ly/2RCjrhg.

16. It is important to clarify that Jamia has started providing reservation to Muslim OBCs and women.

Chapter 6: Muslims as Backward

1. 'Demand to bring Dalit Muslims under the Scheduled Caste category by amending the Constitution', Rajya Sabha Debates, https://bit.ly/2HTQuhf: 'दलित मुसलमान (अरजाल) को अनुसूचित जाति में शामिल करने की मांग गत डेढ़ दशक से की जा रही है। . . . राष्ट्रपति आदेश 1950 के द्वारा इसे केवल हिन्दू दलितों के लिए सीमित कर दिया गया . . . महोदय, मेरा सरकार से निवेदन है कि दलित मुसलमान (अरजाल) को अनुसूचित जाति में शामिल करने के लिए केंद्र सरकार प्रेसिडेंशियल आर्डर 1950 में करते हुए उसमें हिन्दू, सिख एवं नवबौद्ध के साथ मुसलिम शब्द को भी जोड़ें।' https://bit.ly/2N9o6Xs.

2. श्री हुसैन दलवईः सर मेरा एक सवाल है। हमने दलित मुस्लिम और दलित क्रिश्चियन का सवाल उठाया था, इसके उपर आपने कुछ नहीं कहा। https://bit.ly/2tpqKPH.

3. KLS/VNK/1A-11.00/Uncorrected/NotforPublication-08.12.2014, https://bit.ly/2RB2944: 'श्री थावर चन्द गहलोतः सर, निवेदन यह है कि भारत की संवैधानिक व्यवस्था केअंतर्गत जिन वर्गों को अनुसूचित जाति में माना गया है उनमे ये दोनों वर्ग नहीं आते हैं और माननीय उच्चतम न्यायालय मे यह मामला विचाराधीन है। उच्चतम न्यायालय कानिर्णय आने के बाद अगर कोई परिस्थिति होगी तो विचार किया जाएगा, अन्यथा सरकार अभी इस मामले मे सहमत नहीं है।' https://bit.ly/2tpqKPH.

4. Praful Bidwai, 'Combating Muslim exclusion', *Frontline* 23, no. 23 (18 Nov.–1 Dec. 2006), https://bit.ly/2TS5oGm.

5. Emphasis added; *Report of the First Backward Classes Commission*, 1955, p. 27, https://dspace.gipe.ac.in/xmlui/handle/10973/33678.

6. Emphasis added, *Misra Commission Report*, 2007, p. 139, https://bit.ly/2BCsrgZ.

7. Ibid., p. 163.

8. Mohammad Shah, 'State and Violence: The Struggle for Justice and Dignity', *Muslim India* 75 (March 1989): p. 100.

9. Mohammad Shah, 'Reservation for Muslims is Constitutional and Socially Necessary in National Context', *Milli Gazette* (1–15 October 2004): pp. 12–13.

10. 'Resolution of the Muslim Convention for Reservation', 2 February 2009, New Delhi, original emphasis.

11. Mohammad Shah, 'Reservation for Muslims is Constitutional and Socially Necessary in National Context'.

12. Iqbal Ansari, *Political Representation of Muslims of India: 1952–2004* (New Delhi: Manak Publications, 2006).

13. Ibid., Chapter 1.

14. Iqbal Ansari, 'Of Backwardness and Discrimination', *Milli Gazette* (1–15 November 2004).

15. Ibid.

16. Id.
17. Ali Anwar, *Masawat ki Jung: Struggle for Equality* (New Delhi: Indian Social Institute, 2005), Chapters 1 and 3.
18. Anwar, interview by the author, 29 January 2009.
19. Ibid.
20. These three points are taken from a pamphlet entitled *Pichre Vargo ke Arakshan par Khatra*, which was published in the *Pasmanda Awaz* in September–October 2005. These points are not directly mentioned by Anwar; however, he reiterated these concerns in a personal interview with the author on 29 January 2009.
21. Ali Anwar and Yoginder Sikand, 'Ali Anwar's Struggle', CounterCurrents.org, 5 October 2005, https://bit.ly/2V0jZPU.
22. Yoginder Sikand, 'Dalit Muslims', *Outlook*, 20 June 2002, https://bit.ly/2BB5bzW.
23. Ibid.
24. Id.
25. Id.

Chapter 7: The Politics of Triple Talaq

1. 'Objectives', All India Muslim Personal Law Board, https://bit.ly/2HTPRUI.
2. Noorjehan Safia Niaz and Zakia Soman, 'No More "Talaq Talaq Talaq": Muslim Women Call for a Ban on an UnIslamic Practice', Bharatiya Muslim Mahila Andolan, 2015, https://bit.ly/2RF2dzz.
3. Ibid., p. 24.
4. Id., p. 25.
5. Order XXXVIII, S.C.R, 2013, under Article 32 of the Constitution of India, Writ Petition (Civil) 2016, https://bit.ly/2GJfTYB.
6. Counter Affidavit on Behalf of Respondent No. 7, All India Muslim Personal Law Board, Writ Petition (Civil) No. 118 of 2016, https://bit.ly/2IbIxDZ.
7. Ibid.
8. Seema Chishti, 'Austere Ahle Hadees opposes triple talaq but sounds caution', *Indian Express*, 14 October 2016, https://bit.ly/2GkD1g1.
9. Writ Petition (Civil) No. 118 of 2016, https://bit.ly/2GJfTYB.
10. Ibid.

11. Id.
12. Id.
13. Omar Rashid, 'Disturbed by SC order on triple talaq: AIMPLB', *The Hindu*, 22 August 2017, https://bit.ly/2HTUn5P.
14. 'BMMA Reiterates Demand for "Balanced" Muslim Family Law, Hits Out at AIMPLB', Wire, 2 April 2018, https://bit.ly/2UCUXWY.
15. The Muslim Women (Protection of Rights on Marriage) Bill, 2017.
16. Uncorrected Debate, Sixteenth Lok Sabha, https://bit.ly/2DHRv6J.
17. The Muslim Women (Protection of Rights on Marriage) Ordinance, 2018, Section 7a, https://bit.ly/2Nc3wWo, https://bit.ly/2TN4xX7.
18. Ibid., Section 7b.
19. Ibid., Section 7c.

Chapter 8: The New Muslim Elite

1. Syed Zafar Islam, 'A birthday card to the PM', *Indian Express*, 17 September 2018, https://bit.ly/2NmoMfu.
2. Justice Rajindar Sachar, *Social, Economic and Educational Status of the Muslim Community of India: A Report*, Prime Minister's High Level Committee, Cabinet Secretariat, Government of India, November 2006, https://bit.ly/2uOG49P; and Zeeshan Shaikh, 'Ten years after Sachar Report', *Indian Express*, 26 December 2016, https://bit.ly/2GsTaRq.
3. Mohd. Sanjeer Alam, 'Religious and Caste Differentials in Accessing White Collar Jobs in India: Does Education Level the Playing Field?', in *Indian Muslims: Struggling for Equality of Citizenship*, ed. Riaz Hassan (Melbourne: Melbourne University Press, 2016), pp. 94–103.
4. *Sachar Committee Report*, p. 22, https://bit.ly/2POq28L.
5. Naren Karunakaran, 'Muslims constitute 14% of India, but just 3% of India Inc', *Economic Times*, 7 September 2015, https://bit.ly/2G80a69.
6. Pallavi Pundir, 'Aamir Khan on intolerance: Kiran asked me if we should move out of India', *Indian Express*, 24 November 2015, https://bit.ly/2TrSyhH.
7. Prawesh Lama, Twitter post, 24 November 2015, https://bit.ly/2t42mD7.

8. 'Compounding Injustice: The Government's Failure to Redress Massacres in Gujarat', *Human Rights Watch* 15, no. 3 (C) (July 2003), https://bit.ly/2DaZFUF.
9. 'About Us', Indian Muslim Chamber of Commerce and Industry, https://bit.ly/2GoKzOB.
10. Ibid.
11. 'Vision Global', Indian Muslim Chamber of Commerce and Industry, http://www.imcci.net/index.php?link=visionglobal.
12. 'About Us', Association of Muslim Professionals, https://bit.ly/2t7hAXL.
13. 'Vision and Mission', Association of Muslim Professionals, https://bit.ly/2WKgMpg.
14. Madhu Purnima Kishwar, 'Narendra Modi through the Eyes of Gujarati Muslims, Christians', Manushi, Forum for Women's Rights and Democratic Reforms, https://bit.ly/2TT976o.
15. *Sachar Commission Report*, p. 213.

PART III: THE POLITICS OF SIYASI MUSLIMS

Chapter 9: The Metaphors of Muslim Politics: Vote Bank, Good Muslims/Bad Muslims and Muslim Appeasement

1. Deepak Tiwari, 'Votebank politics has destroyed nation like termites: PM Modi', *Week*, 25 September 2018, https://bit.ly/2Bmso91.
2. W.H. Morris-Jones, *Parliament in India* (London and New York: Longman and Green Co., 1957), p. 95.
3. *Report on the First General Elections 1951–52*, Election Commission of India, New Delhi, 1954.
4. S. Gopal, ed., *Selected Works of Jawaharlal Nehru*, vol. 15, part 2 (New Delhi: Jawaharlal Nehru Memorial Fund, 1984), p. 240; and vol. 2, no. 10, pp. 521 and 523.
5. Ibid., p. 240.
6. Ibid.
7. M.N. Srinivas, 'The Dominant Caste in Rampura', *American Anthropologist* 61, no. 1 (February 1959): p. 5.
8. Ibid., p. 15.
9. F.G. Bailey, 'Traditional Society and Representation: A Case Study in Orissa', *European Journal of Sociology* 1, no. 1 (1960): pp. 127.

10. D.L. Seth, 'Political Development of the Electorate', in *Citizens and Parties: Aspects of Competitive Politics in India*, ed. D.L. Seth (New Delhi: Allied Publishers, 1975), pp. 1–2.

11. J.P. Narayan, *A Plea for Reconstruction of Indian Polity* (Kashi: Akhil Bharat Sarv Seva Sangh Prakashan, 1959), p. 75.

12. Jawaharlal Nehru, *Letters to the Chief Ministers: 1947–1964*, vol. 5, ed. G. Parthasarathy (New Delhi: Oxford University Press, 1998), p. 254.

13. Rajani Kothari, *Politics in India* (New Delhi: Orient Longman, 1970), pp. 246–47.

14. 'External forces working against me: PM, PTI', *Times of India*, 15 February 1974, New Delhi, p. 5.

15. Hilal Ahmed, *Muslim Political Discourse in Postcolonial India: Monuments, Memory, Contestation* (London and New Delhi: Routledge, 2014), Chapter 4.

16. Rana Siddiqui Zaman, 'Why "The Sarkari Musalman"?', *National Herald*, 22 October 2018, https://bit.ly/2MOU3Ee.

17. *Selected Works of Jawaharlal Nehru*, vol. 25, p. 227.

18. Emphasis added; Jawaharlal Nehru, *Letters to the Chief Ministers*, vol. 5, p. 457.

19. A.G. Noorani, ed, *The Muslims of India: A Documentary Record* (New Delhi: Oxford University Press, 2003), pp. 183.

20. Hilal Ahmed, 'Understanding postcolonial Muslim politics', *The Hindu*, 30 August 2014, https://bit.ly/2Sutd9B; and Hilal Ahmed, 'A political story of Jama Masjid', *DNA*, 11 November 2014, https://bit.ly/2Bj5dfM.

21. Syed Zafar Islam, 'Why Muslims must give BJP a fair chance', *Indian Express*, 4 May 2017, https://bit.ly/2HDr2w8.

22. 'Mohan Bhagwat says no Hindu Rashtra without Muslims: Is RSS changing before 2019 polls?', ThePrint, 19 September 2018, https://bit.ly/2REUxxt.

23. 'Why Hindu Rashtra: K.S. Sudarshan', Archives of RSS, https://bit.ly/2GbR4Fp.

24. Resolutions: 2011–2020, Archives of RSS, https://bit.ly/1kD7qYm.

25. Emphasis added, Mushirul Hasan, *Legacy of a Divided Nation* (New Delhi: Oxford University Press, 1997), p. 279.

26. 'Sachar Committee: Tell-Tale facts about Muslims in Gujarat: Shri Advani', NarendraModi.in, 17 May 2010, https://bit.ly/2MRJ8JH.

Chapter 10: Muslims and the Future of India's Democracy

1. '"Wherever Muslims Live . . .": Text of Vajpayee's Controversial Goa Speech, April 2002', Wire, 17 August 2018, https://bit.ly/2SfYZYQ.
2. Prime Minister Dr Manmohan Singh, interview by Wolf Blitzer, CNN, 20 July 2005, Ministry of External Affairs, Government of India, https://bit.ly/2X4Z7Jj. This kind of secularism is actually one extreme polarity in this kind of argument.
3. Radhika Ramaseshan, 'Modi chants purification mantra', *Telegraph*, 26 September 2016, https://bit.ly/2WoU0Dy.

Select Bibliography

Ahmad, Imtiaz, ed. *Ritual and Religion among Muslims in India.* New Delhi: Manohar, 1981.

Ahmad, Imtiaz. 'Election Studies in India'. *Economic and Political Weekly* 12, no. 39 (1977): pp. 1677, 1679–680.

Ahmad, Imtiaz. 'Indian Muslims and Electoral Politics'. *Economic and Political Weekly* 2, no. 10 (11 March 1967).

Ahmad, Irfan . *Islamism and Democracy in India: The Transformation of Jamaat-e-Islami.* Princeton: Princeton University Press, 2010.

Ahmed, Hilal. 'Naik, Zakir'. Oxford Islamic Studies Online, https://bit.ly/2I2QMT9.

Ahmed, Hilal. *Muslim Political Discourse in Postcolonial India: Monuments, Memory, Contestation.* London and New Delhi: Routledge, 2014.

Alam, Mohd. Sanjeer. 'Religious and Caste Differentials in Accessing White Collar Jobs in India: Does Education Level the Playing Field?'. In *Indian Muslims: Struggling for Equality of Citizenship.* Edited by Riaz Hassan. Melbourne: Melbourne University Press, 2016.

Ali, Syed Abul Hasan. *Life and Mission of Maulana Mohammad Ilyas.* Lucknow: Academy of Islamic Research & Publications, 2012.

Ambedkar, B.R. *Pakistan or the Partition of India*. Bombay: Thacker & Co. Ltd, 1943.

Anwar, Ali. *Masawat ki Jung: Struggle for Equality*. New Delhi: Indian Social Institute, 2005.

Azad, Maulana Abul Kalam. *India Wins Freedom*. New Delhi: Orient Longman, 1988.

Bajpai, Rochna. *Debating Difference: Group Rights and Liberal Democracy in India*. New Delhi: Oxford University Press, 2012.

Brass, Paul. *Language, Religion and Politics in North India*. Cambridge: Cambridge University Press, 1974.

Brass, Paul. *Language, Religion and Politics in North India*. Cambridge: Cambridge University Press, 1974.

Chakrabarty, Dipesh. '"In the Name of Politics": Sovereignty, Democracy, and the Multitude in India'. *Economic and Political Weekly* 40, no. 30 (23–29 July 2005): pp. 3293–301.

Chatterjee, Partha. *The Nations and Its Fragments: Colonial and Postcolonial Histories*. New Delhi: Oxford University Press, 1993.

Chatterji, Joya. 'South Asian Histories of Citizenship, 1946–1970. *Historical Journal* 55, no. 04 (2012): pp. 1049–071.

Copland, Ian. 'The Princely States, the Muslim League, and the Partition of India in 1947'. *International History Review* 13, no. 1 (1991): pp. 38–69.

Coupland, Reginald. *The Indian Problem: Report on the Constitutional Problem in India*. London and New York: Oxford University Press, 1944.

Faruqi, Ziya-ul-Hasan. *The Deoband School and the Demand for Pakistan*. Calcutta: Asia Publishing House, 1963.

Furber, Holden. 'The Unification of India, 1947–1951'. *Pacific Affair* 24, no. 4 (1951): pp. 352–71.

Gill, Mehar Singh. 'Politics of Population Census Data in India'. *Economic and Political Weekly* 42, no. 3 (20–26 January 2007): pp. 241–49.

Golwalkar, M.S. *Bunch of Thoughts*. Bangalore: Sahitya Sindhu Prakashana, 1966; https://bit.ly/2Bfhh1C.

Guha, Ramachandra. *India after Gandhi: The History of the World's Largest Democracy*. New Delhi: Pan Macmillan India, 2007.

Hasan, Mushirul. 'Adjustment and Accommodation: Indian Muslims after Partition'. *Social Scientist* 18, no. 8/9 (1990): pp. 48–65.

Hasan, Mushirul. 'Muslim Intellectuals, Institutions, and the Post-Colonial Predicament'. *Economic and Political Weekly* 30, no. 47 (1995): pp. 2995–3000.

Hasan, Mushirul. *Legacy of a Divided Nation: India's Muslims since Independence*. London: Hurst & Co., 1997.

Jamaat-e-Islami. 'The Constitution of Jamaat-e-islami Hind'. https://bit.ly/2Iv8e2K.

Kalam, Mohammed A. 'Religious conversions in Tamil Nadu: can these be viewed as protest movements. *Indian Anthropologist* 20, no. 1/2 (1990): pp. 39–48.

Kaviraj, Sudipta. *Imaginary Institution of India: Politics and Ideas.* New York: Columbia University Press, 2010.

Khalidi, Omar. 'From Torrent to Trickle: Indian Muslim Migration to Pakistan, 1947–97'. *Islamic Studies* 37, no. 3 (Autumn 1998): pp. 339–52.

Khan, Maulana Wahiduddin. *Conversion: An Intellectual Transformation.* E-book, https://bit.ly/2SrmflQ.

Khan, Maulana Wahiduddin. *Three Stages of Da'wah Work*. Ebook, https://bit.ly/2DGJ5MM.

Kooiman, Dick. 'Communalism and Indian Princely States: A Comparison with British India'. *Economic and Political Weekly* 30, no. 34 (26 August 1995): pp. 2123–133.

Kothari, Rajni. 'The Congress System Revisited: A Decennial Review'. *Asian Survey* 14, no. 12 (1974): pp. 1035–054.

Kothari, Rajni. *Politics in India*. New Delhi: Orient Longman, 1970.

Krishna, Goral. 'Electoral Participation and Political Integration'. *Economic and Political Weekly* 2, no. 3/5 (February 1967): pp. 179–81, 183–85, 187–90.

Madani, Arshad, and Quaran Sharif Muhammad. *Anuwad aur Vyakhya*. New Delhi: Jamiat Ulama e-Hind, 1992.

Mahmood, Tahir. *Minorities Commission 1978–2015: Minor Role in Major Affairs*. New Delhi: LexisNexis-Universal, 2016.

Malik, Jamal. 'A.H. Ali Nadwi'. In *Historical Thinking in South Asia: A Handbook of Sources from Colonial Times to the Present*. Edited by Michael Gottlob. New Delhi: Oxford University Press, 2003.

Malik, Jamal. *Islam in South Asia: A Short History*. New Delhi: Orient BlackSwan, 2012.

Maududi, Abul Ala. *A Historic Address at Madras*. Translated by Mohammad Siddiqui Naveed. New Delhi: Markazi Maktaba Islami Publishers, 2009.

Maududi, Abul Ala. *Pavitr Quran*. New Delhi: MMI, 1970.

Metcalf, Barbara D. 'Living Hadith in the Tablīghī Jama'āt'. *Journal of Asian Studies* 52, no. 03 (1993): pp. 603–05.

Metcalf, Barbara D., and Husain Ahmad Madani. *The Jihad for Islam and India's Freedom*. Oxford: Oneworld Publications, 2008.

Morris-Jones, W.H. *Parliament in India*. London and New York. Longmans, Green and Co., 1957.

Nadwi, Abul Lais Islahi. *Bharat ka Navnirman Aur Hum (Rebuilding of India and Our Role)*. Translated by Afzal Husaain. New Delhi: Markazi Maktaba Islami Publishers, 2014.

Nadwi, Syed Abul Hasan Ali. *Appreciation and Interpretation of Religion in the Modern Age*. Translated by Syed Athar Husain. Lucknow: Academy of Islamic Research & Publications, 1980.

Nadwi, Syed Abul Hasan Ali. *Hindustani Musalman Ek Drishti Mein (An Overview of Indian Muslims)*. New Delhi: Markazi Maktaba Islami Publishers, 2014.

Nadwi, Syed Abul Hasan Ali. *Inviting to the Way of Allah*. London: Ta-Ha Publishers Ltd and UK Islamic Academy, 1992.

Nadwi, Syed Abul Hasan Ali. *Live to Lead: A Call to Indian Muslims*. Translated by Shah Ebadur Rahman. Lucknow: Academy of Islamic Research &Publications, 1980.

Nadwi, Syed Abul Hasan Ali. *Muslims in India*. Translated by Mohammad Asif Kidwai. Lucknow: Academy of Islamic Research & Publications, 1976.

Nadwi, Syed Abul Hasan Ali. *Try to Understand the Problems and Sentiments of Indian Muslims: A Prerequisite for Peaceful Co-existence*. Lucknow: All India Solidarity Forum, N.D.

Nigam, Aditya. 'A Text without Author: Locating Constituent Assembly as Event'. *Economic and Political Weekly* 39, no. 21 (2004): pp. 2107–113.

Noorani, A.G. 'Patel's communalism—a documented record'. *Frontline*, 13 December 2013, https://bit.ly/2GDigwR.

Noorani, A.G., ed. *The Muslims of India: A Documentary Record*. New Delhi: Oxford University Press, 2003.

Oommen, John. 'Politics of Communalism in Kerala'. *Economic and Political Weekly* 30, no. 11 (18 March 1995): pp. 544–47.

Pandey, Gyanendra. 'Can a Muslim be an Indian?' *Comparative Studies in Society and History* 41, no. 4 (1999): pp. 608–29.

Phillips, Anne. *The Politics of Presence*. Oxford: Clarendon Press, 1995.

Pirzada, Syed Sharifuddin. *Foundation of Pakistan: All India Muslim League Documents (1906–1941), Vol. 2*. Karachi: National Publishing House, 1970.

Qasmi, Mufti Mohammad Roshan Shah. *Malfoozat wa Iqtebasaat Maulana Mohammad Yusuf Kandhlawi*. New Delhi: Rashid Publications, N.D.

Roger, Jeffery, and Jeffery Patricia. 'Saffron Demography, Common Wisdom, Aspirations and Uneven Governmentalities'. *Economic and Political Weekly* 40, no. 5 (2005): pp. 447–53.

Sachchidananda. 'Sociology of National Integration'. *Bulletin of the Deccan College Research Institute* 31/32, no. 1/2 (1970–71/1971–72): pp. 193–201.

Shahabuddin, Syed. 'Sachar Report: Analyses of Approach and Strategy'. *Muslim India* 271 (January 2007).

Shaikh, Farzana. *Community and Consensus in Islam: Muslim Representation in Colonial India, 1860–1947*. Cambridge: Cambridge University Press, 1991.

Shakir, Moin. *Muslims in Free India*. New Delhi: Kalamkar Prakashan Pvt. Ltd, 1972.

Sikand, Yoginder. 'Arya Shuddhi and Muslim Tabligh: Muslim Reactions to Arya Samaj Proselytization (1923–30)'. In *Religious Conversion in India: Modes, Motivations, Meanings*, edited by Rowena Robinson and Sathianathan Clarke. New Delhi: Oxford University Press, 2003.

Smith, W.C. 'Hyderabad: Muslim Tragedy'. *Middle East Journal* 4, no. 1 (January 1950): pp. 27–51.

Troll, Christian W. 'Two Conceptions of Da'wá in India: Jamā'at-i Islāmi and Tablīghī Jamā'at'. *Archives de sciences sociales des religions*, 39e Année, No. 87(1994): pp. 115–33.

Wright, Theodore P. 'Muslim Legislators in India: Profile of a Minority Elite'. *Journal of Asian Studies* 23, no. 2 (1964): pp. 253–67.

Wright, Theodore P. 'The Muslim League in South India since Independence: A Study in Minority Group Political'. *American Political Science Review* 60, no. 3 (September 1966): pp. 579–99.

Zaman, Muhammad Qasim. *The Ulama in Contemporary Islam: Custodians of Change*. Princeton and Oxford: Princeton University Press, 2007.

Zamindar, Vazira F. *The Long Partition and the Making of Modern South Asia: Refugees, Boundaries, Histories*. New York: Penguin Viking, 2007.

Index

Sudarshan News, 30
Sunni, Sunni Islam, Sunnis, 38,
    45, 132, 156
    da'wa movements, 57
    Muslims of Hanafi Shariat,
        127–28
    and Shias, 20, 33
Supreme Court
    conceptualizes
        'distinctiveness, 92
    judgement on teen talaq,
        132–39
    symbols of Muslimness, 4

Tablighi Jamaat, 38, 39, 45, 47,
    49, 50–52, 53, 61, 156
Tafrigh-i waqt (sparing time), 50
Tafseer, 21
Taliban, 188
territorial nationalism, 47
terrorism, Islamic terrorism,
    xxxvii, 59, 78, 144
    and Pakistan's involvement in
        Kashmir, 78
Thackeray, Bal, 72
tolerance/intolerance controversy,
    151–52
triple talaq, politics of, xix, xxxvii,
    xxx, 25, 191, 193
    and multiple choice question
        (MCQ), 125–28 Muslim
        contestations on, 128–32
    punishment to Muslim men,
        139–42
    Shah Bano case, xxviii, 45,
        137, 139, 176, 184–85,
        193

Supreme Court judgement,
    132–39
Turkman Gate, xxvii

Ulema class, 21, 47, 126, 132,
    137, 142, 156, 180, 191
unemployment, xvii, 146
Uniform Civil Code (UCC), 126,
    129, 131, 184
United Progressive Alliance
    (UPA), xxx, xxxi, 84, 96, 97,
    163, 176, 183, 189
    UPA 1 and 2, 84, 176
universal adult franchise, 19
universal reservation, theory of,
    110
unorganized sector, 146
untouchability, untouchables, 104,
    105–06
Upadhyaya, Deen Dayal, xxxiii,
    70–71, 163, 189
Urdu, 25, 52, 53
    decline of, 57
Uttar Pradesh: Assembly
    elections, 2016, 195

Vajpayee, A.B., xxiv, xxx, 188
Vande Mataram, xix, xxxix, 77, 79
Vedic Saptasindhus, 67
Verma, Justice J.S., 73
victimhood of Muslims, xxxiv–xxxv,
    101, 144, 156, 185–86, 191
violence against Muslims, 193–94,
    198
violence and Jihad, xviii
Vishwa Hindu Parishad (VHP),
    xxvi, xxvii, 31, 69